*keeping
alive!*

Ragpicking Ezekiel's Bones

Pamela L. Sumners

3/15/21

Cover Art:
UNTITLED
by Paul G. Sumners/Silvergel/Paul Sumners Photography

Back Cover Photo: George W. Sumners

Book Design by:

UnCollected Press
8320 Main Street, 2nd Floor
Ellicott City, MD 21043

For more books by UnCollected Press:
www.therawartreview.com

First Edition 2020
ISBN: 978-1-71668-084-7

ACKNOWLEDGMENTS AND THANKS

Lovingly dedicated to **Liz Hubertz**, my wife, by acclamation the finest person on the planet. She deserves her own page but she's an environmental lawyer, and I don't want to be scolded about wasting trees.

Grateful acknowledgment to Paul G. Sumners, for the photographs appearing on the cover and to all of the editors and staff of literary reviews in which these poems previously appeared, sometimes with slight editorial changes to the author's text that appears here:

The American Journal of Poetry, Bangalore Review, BACOPA, Bayou Magazine, Better than Starbucks, Blue Unicorn, Brushfire, California Quarterly, A Crossfire of Winds, december magazine, Eunoia Review, Galway Review, Genre Urban Arts, Gival Press, Green Light Review, Gyroscope, Halcyone/Black Mountain Press 64 Best Anthology, Halfway Down the Stairs, Haunted Waters Press, Heartland Review, Heirlock, High Shelf Press, Hole in the Head Review, The Lake, Loch Raven Review, Midwest Review, Mudlark, Muse Pie/Shot Glass, New Verse News, New Voices Project, New Millennium/Sunspots, Public Poetry, Raw Art Review, Snakeskin Poetry Blog, Showbear Family Circus, Streetlight Magazine, Tahoma Literary Review, Third Wednesday, 34th Parallel, Twisted Vine, UCity Review, V Press, Valley Voices, Voices of Eve, The Voices Project, W.B. Yeats Society, What Rough Beast, Worcester Review, Woven Tale Press.

I am also very appreciative of the production and clerical help of Kelli Gardner, Liz Hubertz, and especially LaRetha Johnson (my savior!) in organizing/formatting so many of the submissions for the journals listed above and the poems in this volume, and of course, to Henry Stanton, editor of UnCollected Press which brings you this collection. Not a lot of editors, journals, or presses care much about MFA-less, unconventional, often vernacular writers who blend formalism with free verse. Thanks to Henry for welcoming the literary vagabonds of contemporary writing, giving the pariahs a platform and a home—poets like me.

Personal gratitude to the physicians, nurses, and medical staff who saved my life, and to my 2019 organ donor—all made this publication possible.

Please note that these poems were written in 8.5x11 format. Pamela Sumners sometimes writes in very long lines by contemporary standards. Please read them for rhythm and disregard harsh or odd line breaks necessitated by formatting her lines for 6x9 dimensions.

*These poems are not to be presumed to be based on true events and may represent fiction. Names, characters, and incidents may be a memory play, and therefore tinged with blue light. Resemblance to actual events, places, or people, living or dead, may be the product of artful imagination or entirely coincidental.

Table of Contents

FORSYTHIA (in a Southern climate)

I have no money on your birthday,
so I stole you a branch of forsythia.
If ever a flower speaks for itself, is the
res ipsa loquitur of shrubbery,
it's forsythia, curling from the little live wires
it threads, puffing its blazing breath forward,
a mutable fire, this flaming yellow
dipping a summer toe into autumn,
fall to fall, limp but insouciant.
This little spark wants to set kindling
to winter. A man named Fortune
discovered it, described it as a stalk-scented
star-flower. It's a cusp plant, just as
your birthday bridges the summer to fall.

I leave no note with it, because it has no need
of words that, like underbellies of leaves,
turn on you, trembling, spiraling
to earth already compost, soft rot,
an undertow dragging you aground.
Words aren't for birthdays anyway because they
give mainly to the giver who hears himself
imagining your thanks. Forsythia
brushes off its praise, squatting in
its comfortable, plain-talk splendor.
It has that shy rube-like modesty,
cooing "Aw, shucks" to compliments.
The Victorians called it *forsythia suspena*,
for hopeful anticipation, and surrounded
its four-pronged petals with baby's breath
and Queen Anne's lace for birthing bouquets.
When the eyes blazed open the baby saw flower

1

and star both, in one look. Like when I see you,
whole earth and sky in one look, wordlessly.

FOR YOUR LEAVING

It's a nice night for trains,
for traveling,
for insects that fly by the stars,
but I know nothing of trains.
I know the long solemn tracks
that unfold for me in my long dreams,
and in my long dreams I have paused
for that pedestrian love
which should never have overtaken me
at the crossing gates of this (my brief
my little) life, but poets I think
should know something of trains.
So I listen. I watch the tracks.
My great grandfather, they say,
built the tunnel through Lookout Mountain
sheltering tracks that ran
from Chattanooga to Vicksburg
and during the Civil War
Bragg's men fought off the blue
in the tunnel my very Southern
Alabama rebel ancestor built.
But that is all my knowledge of trains.

I have stood by Moccasin Bend
and dreamed of heroes on the tracks
and wished I had made this river,
laid these tracks, with my body
for a spade hollowed limestone
and left my purpled shadow dying
on the walls of the tunnel.

I have prayed for some knowledge

of trains, of journeys, prayed
and strained to hear the sound of the tracks:
dissonance and steel.
If I knew of trains I might know
why you watched your dreams
blast-capping themselves, might
drive the spike of some better lines
for you. But I am ignorant.
Nevertheless this is for you;
my seal is on it, plain and frank,
like you. These words are not praise
dropped in the church-plate for guilt's
sake, but well-spaced ties, because
the audacity of your fiber
flows into me like dreams, or rivers.
We will make our way alone, carving lives
from piles of tar-pitched timbers and stone.
I give you this because your bones
have a typography theirs alone. They make
me wish I were a traveler of trains,
an architect of tunnels or possibly
some bright fixed point in the heavens
decisively spinning its mortality out,
coming again and again to dragoon passengers
through storms and lead them through the dark,
a conductor of trains, arranging our destinies
along these tracks, always going at night, following
the lead-car headlight of our brightness gleaming,
ignoring the vicarious freeloader of a
river that runs below alongside our route.
We would know only urgency and longing.

I know nothing of the greater urgency
and secrecy of trains, why they go at night,

but I have heard that once in Arkansas a maniac
was almost caught by the police even
as the train came by, that he escaped
by jumping over the tracks just before it came,
over the tracks and into the swamp.
So I know a little of the saving grace
of trains, how they take pity sometimes
on the pursued and the pursuer and
sometimes leave us to breathe
our own days to their deaths, in muffled
sleep, to bear alone the slow progress
through clutches of loblolly, hearing lonesome
hushed continuities of winds in trees.
I do know a little piece, enough, perhaps.
I know that sometimes, left prostrate
by so many choices, a train can come.

In the season of my innocence
I have played chase with trains, played Christ
with trains, asking if there is a way
for one to pass me by, a way to jump
in front of it and cross to the other side,
to hear the crack of my foot on leaves
on the safe side of the tracks
and know that it is past, that every sound
of leap and branch pronounces the shortness of time.
I wish trains had never stopped to claim me.
I wish I had never thought of trains,
never known grief, never despised
this self-eating depravity of passion.
But that is not the nature of trains
or a watcher of trains; we must
follow the little length of lonely track
just ahead and not wish to have made it.

We must be blameless and we must not blame.
I don't blame you, boarder of trains,
night-traveler. I make my little peace
if you will take a little pity.

SKIPPING ROCKS

On Easter, after all the dyed eggs had dried for your hunt
and the Easter Bunny had come with his loot to sweeten
your breakfast as the stone still blocked our Arimethean door,
you put on your Oxford cloth and blazer for the service
of the high-church Episcopalians my people called gutter
Catholics just like they called the Unitarians atheists
in search of the remote possibility that there is a god.

You took communion with the flippant contempt of a
boy throwing stubbed cigarette butts in the offering plate.

The church is convenient for neighborhood Christianity,
being just around the block so we don't have far to walk
in dress shoes and we don't stain our fancy jackets with
too much sweat toward piety. After church you said,
I like Christmas better; no one dies in that story, and
went back home, to this place where I knew that
happiness unhappened, knowing, like I know the Easter
ending, that I bought this house, out of pity, from a woman
who inherited four nieces to stack in these dark corners
after a no-good brother-in-law beat her sister to death.

We see alcoves here we don't visit, phantoms that life
never did inhabit, trashy recesses that won't stay clean.

For this, out of pity, I paid full price. Bored, oppressed
by the weight of air in this house, as sturdy and remorseless
as its age in unloving hands, we left for the park and
I taught you to skip rocks, thinking how our house
skips nothing, leaving ripples all the same. Your image
in the water wavered, I heard the glide and plunk of rocks,
a perceptual entropy, the price of living here, of all places,

7

ringing the registers of what will be memory, cashing us out
to our last blasphemous tithe, stone by stone.

TANGLED

My home is a living drive-through cathedral, limp Spanish moss
and kudzu its Sistine dome.
This land was made for driving, for Kings of Tupelo with fins and
white-wall wings and a Southern woman's arm dangling its
boneless fragility from the window, like they do in these parts.

Every road is a pulsing artery to towns named Damascus, Smyrna,
Philadelphia, Corinth, Shiloh, Southern fried chicken on Sunday
towns where even the Episcopalians rumble the Lord's Word
with the brimstone Baptists' hairlip-like precision and there is
supper on the grounds (dinner if you're all puffed-up and strutting
your fancy pants), with ambrosia and seafoam salad desserts.

My father whipsawed us between the dazzling dogwood
of Tennessee, the hot ore and hot temper of the Big Bad 'Ham,
the grizzled old Arkansas Ozarks jutting up like dinosaur teeth.
His father named his Ishmael and expected him not to wander,
leaving us rootless memories of the patriarch who wanted to be
called Daddy. A dinner on the grounds sort, I called him Father.

He taught us the various routes to "the country" in Sylacauga,
not a romantic place, no noble Creek or Cherokee translation:
just "The Place of the Chalaka Tribe" where the only known
meteor strike that killed somebody occurred, hurled down from
pre-history, finding its target smack between Vincent and
 Childersburg.

Father would sneak up on Sylacauga through the Jim Nabors
 "Gomer" Highway, or if you drove from Tennessee, past the
faded, handpainted billboards of Nickerson Farms bragging on its
famous pecan divinity and the Fort Payne KKK welcoming you
to the flaming heart of Dixie (or--you never knew) sometimes

9

we might take the Jim Lindsey "Goober" Highway. You could pluck
  out
a route from Chickamauga straight to the country people in
  Sylacauga.
With the country cousins in Sylacauga you might strip a wheat-like
  grass
of its curled brown leaves, light them with your parents' matches
  and
smoke them, calling it Indian tobacco. You might break the stems
  and
peel out the white center: "Indian gum." It tasted like Styrofoam
  but fed
imagination. Bad things can happen in Sylacauga, too, the
  palpable, sulfuric
stench of the paper mills drenching the Confederate jasmine, the
  acrid
blossoms of their emissions turning the sky as gray as waves of
  the returning
Glorious Dead, as gray as the coal and ore miners wracked with
  poverty and
pellagra. These are the gray men, the dead men, the men caught
  up in miasmic,
not Corinthian, skies. The Big Mules have had their way with both
  earth and air.

The country holds specters, shadow-ashes slashed into photo
  paper, curling edges
of memory. I recall a picture of me leaning on our sleek-
silhouetted Buick
that darted through the backroads to come to rest at the
  honeysuckle hedges.
In my mint chiffon and tulle Easter dress, my thighs squeezed
  tight, my butt pressed

with hold-your-breath grit, afraid that any minute my control
  would fragment and
I'd look down on my flooded patent leather shoes spilling over the
  Sylacauga sediment,
dodging gravel bombs thrown by a vicious cousin we saw as a
  waste of chromosomes—
that I would melt like "McArthur Park" sweet green vinyl grooves
  into Sylacauga ochre,
me giving way to my breaking levee of bladder, drowning in a
  hurricane of little-girl pee.
I tangled my dress on the Buick's bumper, bringing all the women
  like swarming fire ants,
clucking about whether my pastel Easter best could be mended.
  All wanted to throw the miscreant in Grandmother's jail, an old
  barn by the fetid hoof-and-mouth pond.

. . .

My doctors, poking around my belly with scalpels, cameras,
  gloved, mysterious hands
discover that I am a medical freak. Most umbilical cords snip
  and cap themselves,
but mine kept growing, settling into my viscera, wrapping into my
  vascular system
like the braided vines we used to swing over dry creek beds thirty
  feet below us, launching
to the bluff on the other side. Or maybe it had built itself into an
  Ionic column, propping
up all my veins, letting them cling like the gully swinging vine. It
  has grown into my DNA,
the floral sprays, the lazy days with Indian gum in the shimmering
  heat, tea made in jugs
with two cups of sugar, snapping purple-hull peas on the peeling,
  warped wood porches
at the country peoples' houses, estates named after the number

of oaks on the dirt road,
a green neon sign leading you in flashing lights to visit "Our Brand
New Mausoleum" in a
cedar-framed cemetery, tires burning with the rubbery olfactory
assault of a paper mill,
childhood maids named Eula Mae, Eula Fay, Lula Mae, Esther
Mae, the women who raised
the South's white children with their tangled loyalties, tangled
roots, intertwined viscera.
These serial Eula-maids, silenced by courtrooms and ballot boxes,
smoothed out the cuffs
on a favorite cardigan, laid them out so we could slip comfortably
into our casual racism.

And I know now, gnashing at a legal brief in the Pell City
Courthouse, that these same women
trusted with the towheads of the South, our maids, could not
testify there. They could drink
from the "Colored" fountain, marked in Art Deco letters that have
been removed, but their
stain comes through. They paint over the sun-faded shadow-
letters, whitewashing the wall.
You can't erase what has been written in blood. You can't pluck
out an umbilical guy wire
anchoring what sends our lifeblood, diffuses it in our bodies,
cannot suppress these hieroglyphs
any more than we can mask the sulfur smell of paper mills with
the sickly scent of gardenias.
This constellation knitted itself into an Eden with Satan and Jesus
wrapped around the same
magnolia, content with the roots but still haggling over an apple
while giving an ovation to the sky.
Your two-lane highways, your Appalachia, Ozarks, Smokies, your
veins pulsing history and ore

are still close in rear-view mirrors as this rough beast slouches toward Birmingham to be reborn.

BIRMINGHAM'S GOOD GLASS EYE

Capote had a glass harp.
Poe had a tell-tale heart.
Hitchcock had a glass eye,
just like Mother's husband.

He popped it out to "rest my eye"
and put it in his three-legged smoking
bowl, butternut pine with spindled legs.

"No lady smokes on the street," Mother says.

The glass eye stares at you in silent reproach.
Sometimes it rolls for awhile in its bowl.
Sometimes it rests under his Post-Herald
topping the bowl, like it's reading the news.

Mother says he lost that eye in World War II.

She drags on her Parliament, nestled near his Kents,
Real slow as she watches the Lawrence Welk Show.
The glass eye blinks at the flickering blue glow.

You still check sidewalk butts for lipstick prints.

STARS FELL ON ALABAMA AT VINCENT HIGH SCHOOL

My father was far short of 5-10,
but I thought he was tall enough
to take a slingshot to the sun if
it was too hot. That didn't begin
to explain the blooming sweat spots
in the pits of his short-sleeved shirts
that moored paisley ties and pen clips.

My father could shoot down anything—
the stars, the sky, the whole Mason-Dixon
line with his Willy Loman Ball mason jar
in Grandmother's backyard, seeking solace
in arguments about Gubner George Wallace
and upping the Blue Book value of school
busing for his audience under that pin oak.

He turned down a Miata deal, bought Renault,
and went broke. He bought Kaiser aluminum
cars made in Chile and Li'l Abner amusement
parks. But to the end of his salesman's days
he remembered the hot haze of an Alabama
September night, not the inquisitions into
his business decisions. He remembers the gasped
derision of his peers that one time, that one time

with the pass blooming into a clear interception
that he batted down instead. He argued it out
for 40 years with himself, replaying his blown shot,
hearing the jeers at this lost chance, the whole field
his for a quick catch and a sauntering prance. This looming
regret in the air made him taller than he was.

SOUTHERN LICKS

We call all the dogs by the wrong names now we've had so many.
A Southern tongue says it like that and skips modifiers and
glosses over comma splices unpausing like rocks only briefly
suspended in breathless skipping over all these pitiful little
childhood creeks chock full of crawdads that seemed rivers then.

A Southern pause, caught in a catgotyourtongue small
social pratfall, licks its lips and purrs "You're so sweet" or
"Aren't you just too precious?" with murderous intent,
impaling you on the little unliquored olive fork of compulsive
cordiality. Welcome to hell, y'all come in now because we've
baked you a pie and a nice broccoli and belladonna casserole
I was going to take to church, but here you are, and bless your
 heart
honey I don't mean to be ugly but I never really pictured pastels
for your color palate. Well, bless your little ole pea-pickin'
heart anyway. Through every mesh and aluminum hydraulic
spring porch door coiled to strike and hit you where the good
Lord split you on your way out, I've sulked and watched and
taken Dixie plates of fried chicken home for the drive to cities
mammoth as Big Bad Birmingham. I have forgotten the art
of remembering dog names, names of in-laws, the "shewuzza"* to
family-tree cousins by marriage and call everyone out of their
 names.

But they were precious, they were sweet, wilting in the heat with
ice tea or washtub-size water bowls and they were fiercely here
once, piddling the floor, barking at shadows, half-knowing
 strangers.

_____

* "Shewuzza," as in "she was a" [maiden name] before she married and
took her husband's surname.

16

Turn on the porchlight so that night moths can die Daedalus,
touching Orion's belt and not the ornery sun, bless their hearts.

LAST RITES

It rained cottonmouths for 30 days after you died.
They wore proud boots and took over the streets,
slithered and kicked through the steel-plated doors.
They sat coiled or casually drooped in your special recliner.
They ate the last Tyson's chicken in Arkansas—they did!
and then ravaged the okra and bean patches out back.
Then they took the tomatoes and purple-hull peas,
cutting a swath like Sherman's army marching to sea.

Their white mouths turned a deep heliotrope purple.
We plied them with offerings of heavy red wine
and they turned all purple and died. We swept snakeskins
for weeks. Next the bats came, echolocating what we
humans heard only as a series of slight erratic clicks.
We developed a decoder that could read bat-tongue for us
and learned that they repeated through the walls a gossip chorus:
"You know he heard the wind chimes just before he died, a music
that played so hauntingly on the listening ears of time."

We banged every pot and pan in the house like a marching band
starting off a Fourth of July parade with John Phillip Souza's brass
until they gave up roost, a lonely, leaning excuse for a
 chimney.
When finally we wept and muttered a flood of desolate words
over your cavernous deep rhombus in the earth, a dark hole
 really,
an aunt we barely knew said to me, "Give me your last skinny-
 back
wishbone hug and tell us how thin we've become."

THE ONLY SAFE JAR OF MAYONNAISE IN ALABAMA

My mother loved mohair so much
She took plastic wrap and covered it up.
My mother had seven fur coats.
In July in Birmingham, lush to the touch.

In her fur July Alabama hothouse pouch
She coddled that jar like she did her mohair couch.
It was 12 ounces of bliss toted like a love note,
Pure, unpoisoned, tamper-proof cardiac mulch.

My mother festooned herself in her best jewels
Because we all know that yardwork has grooming rules,
And they include mink and mayo to soothe your throat.
Of course you've hosed your garden tools before use.

Mother tells you not to sleep with men you're not married to
And you hear this as not hustlin' people strange to you
Even if you do got a two-piece custom-made pool cue*
While you guard that Hellmann's like Titanic's last lifeboat.

---

* Jim Croce, "You Don't Mess Around with Slim."

MY MOTHER'S GUEST ROOM

My mother had a guest room but no guests,
a large collection of regrets bereft of reason.
She was not used to the ordinary nicety
of owning a room, having lived at Bryce
for two decades. This ugly Irondale ranch
with its knotty pine was her new asylum
since, where the deranged pin oak scratched
the guest room screens and beat them like Bedlam
when the skies retched and hail pinged its branches.

The guest room she reserved for the wandering
ghosts of five children she'd very seldom seen
over 20 years, but she preserved each by swaddling
Christmas presents here, under all their names, leaving
cantilevered spires of packages, floor to ceiling.

I visited once, in the charge of two much older brothers
who ridiculed her crazy talk until I cried inconsolably.
Abashed, they tried to smooth my ruffled little-girl feathers
by prescribing me two tumblers of straight barley whiskey.
I could not have been 12 on that morose trip to Mother's.

My mother gave me a garishly foiled Christmas present then,
and I was sure that submerged below the shiny bows and wrap
lurked a set of serial killer baseball cards with handy hygiene
and clean-up tips from them. But she'd just strapped
lacy pink silk pajamas she'd bought on discount at Parisian's
to an ostrich feather boa and some random purple mittens.

No one ever knew what quiescently frozen confections
glazed to make the blind curves of Mother's mind so treacherous,
the little currents of her thoughts all frost-fog advection

skimming a fetid pond, hiding under wraps things too dangerous
to know, such as that she witnessed the time Judas Iscariot
came to charcoal-etch the headstones in our rakish family plot.

She ghosted the discount racks year-round for 20 Christmases
she was kept in a cinder room at Bryce, shut away from all of us.
When she glided through Five Points South mall, she spread her
rod like Moses, parting crowds, discordantly chanting under her
 breath
*"To market, to market, to buy a fat hog. Home again home again,
Jiggety jog."*

(SUPPOSING) MY MOTHER WAS A BLUE HERON

I.

My mother was a blue heron who blew in off the Delta
in a hurricane and wound up land-locked in Alabama
surrounded by red clay and peaches and zigzag fences
somewhere between the Romulus and Remus of almost-
central Alabama, Jemison and Clanton. My father was
your ordinary earthbound swain, and together they
accumulated memories to feather their imperiled nest
the way limestone cliffs alluviate dehydrated lichen.
He bound her feet to the stone to keep her at home where
they gave birth to five ugly ducklings, or perhaps five
red herrings, or maybe five black sheep whose mother
thought they were all the first lambs of spring but not
at all fit for slaughter. She thought they were the very first.

***

My mother was the hurricane that blew the blue heron
over the bridge that was my father, and in that storm
she spawned five tornadoes that tore up all the trailer parks
and knocked the battle-flagged dome off the Capitol building,
bringing in five separate thunderstorms that washed out all
the gutters and left trash walking in riding boots on the streets
of Birmingham, Montgomery, all the way to Ohio and Chicago.
My mother was the hurricane of many names bearing down
on all the levees but my mother had no calm still eye.
My mother was a cyclone, a full force gale, unbuilding things,
washing away sandbags, but she herself was never thrown,
because she stood one-legged, the other tied to a stone.

***

Suppose that my father was a swan and the swan was called
Zeus, and that I do not have a mother at all but sprang straight
from my father's head, full-grown and fully blown from his
 laureled
godhead, and that we glide and glide together on lakes of
 obsidian,
eating the ambrosia that rains across the wilderness, rains down
from the quartermasters at Mount Olympus. Suppose that my
 father
was a swan. Suppose that he glides and glides in his own
 reflection.

My mother was a blue heron. My father was Zeus, within her
 wingspan.

II.

Supposing that my mother was the Gingerbread Woman, iced and
 frosted
and that she buttoned up her jacket and set her raisin eyes
 homeward and that
she ran whee whee whee all the way home, to her licorice-
 scented gingerbread
house near the river and my father chased her all the way there,
 stubbing a
toe in the water, and that he started to melt. He melted until he
 lost a leg but
still they had five ginger snaps that burned the mouths of their
 lovers from
Birmingham bars to Michigan Avenue van der Rohe corporate
 mousetrap
cubicles but every Mother's Day, Mother got five fresh bouquets

of snapdragons.
Father thought the snap children were not quite done, and were
 raw inside
but Mother kept them warm in parchment skins and pronounced
 them crisp, perfect.
Two turned blond as sand dollars and three stayed the russet of
 their birth
and built their own gingerbread houses right down the street
 where Mother
and Father ran and ran and Father melted as he ran and mother
 smiled a frosted
smile at him. My father was a one-legged gingerbread man who
 ran until he
caught her and set her up in her gingerbread house with
 peppermint shingles
and bitter anise trim. Suppose that five ginger snaps grew into
 crumbling,
hard-bitten lives after leaving Mother's pungent house but it still
 was perfect.

III.

Suppose my mother was a blue whale and that my father was
 oracle-eyed Jonah.
She was out for a casual stroll in the same old neighborhood, so
 she yawned
and drew my father in whole, where in her belly he acquired
 tastes of Biblical
proportions and took in prophecies of heaven and changed them
 into intimations
of despair. He dreamed in there of a chariot hell-bent on the
 firmament that would
let him rise like Elijah, up and out of the belly of this beast.

In my huge blue mother he was sentient but mute, wishing for the
gift of ventriloquism
to hurl his prophecies forward past her viscous entrails. He
wondered whether God
gave him the short end of the stick when He made His prophet His
pensioner,
surviving on nothing but Mother's indigestible bits and the timely
repentant
expedient of prayer. While he was in there, God imprinted in him
the sacred grief
of the aggrieved, apoplectic priest and that of the eternally
temporizing penitent,
there in the slimy belly of the beast. He slept in there with a wall-
eyed stare,
tossing in his doomsday dreams of Nineveh, Thebes, thinking
unawares of
Nebuchadnezzer's mess halls, curious writings on the walls,
hieroglyphs drawn
from the mouths of babes, of griefs in the lions' den for a
prophet's shattered peace.

My mother tired of his wrathful sleeps, his tossing in his bunk,
found him too unsavory
even for her bilious entrails, was bored that he was doomed to
compose jeremiads
about his disappointment and hunger. So my mother spewed him
and ejected
with him five sententious serpents born with guns and spears
instead of arms and hands,
and Father named each and every one of them for a mad captain
named Ahab, but
Mother played with them in the waves, tossing them from time to
time in the air.
When they misbehaved as children will, she rapped their guns

with a spar and trimmed their spears to toothpicks.
These mad captains would blubber after her, struggling fruitlessly
to capture her full attention and to learn her name.

My mother was a blue whale. My father was a prophet who saw
 in a vision
five sermonizing sea snakes, born in God's image, their mother's
 perfection.

IV.

My mother was a through-the-glass darkly blue-tinted mirror with
 a whalebone handle.
My father, always standing behind her like a stalker, cast his
 reflection forward
and its ugliness shattered the glass. My mother, not one to waste
 things because
squanderings always count, scooped up five slices of glass in her
 ungloved hands,
bloodying herself in their handling. The five shards were born with
 telescopic vision
that left them prone to punishment because they always threw
 light when they were told
to leave the dark corners alone. But Mother thought they were
 perfect, so jagged and so
shiny. Bright and sharp, all the teachers wrote on their
 deportment cards. All her
fragile fractiles shattered again, casting their father's reflection
 over their shoulders
from Red Mountain to Lakeshore Drive, glinting in the sun, glaring
 in the snow. They
shimmered like diamonds cast into the sand, dangerously
sparkling at strangers.

V.

My mother was a riverboat that ran up to the bluffs by the
  melancholy Natchez Trace
and sometimes picked up passengers like my prophetic peg-
  legged gingerbread father
who was either a gambler or a drowning washed-up riverboat
  captain whose boat he'd
let run aground when his drunken sailors hit a sand bar at Pas
  Christian. He called the dice
five times at the roulette wheel and Mother said he always bet
  against the house but that
it was perfect, just perfect that way. Five die rolled themselves
  through life like it was
Russian roulette. They kept Mother in perfect suspense, but she
  was well-moored and
never was tossed or troubled. The gingerbread captain had
  anchored her with a stone.

VI.

My mother was a blue-blooded mermaid who swam out of the
  sea oats at Mobile Bay.
My father was the Minotaur who found her there, washed ashore
  and flailing. He split
her tail so she could be taught to walk on land but she always
  precariously tottered
like a footbound Mandarin courtesan. My father thought this was
  just as well because
she was too beautiful to let her get away. It was just as well that
  she stayed, now that
she walked on land. They had five mermaid-Minotaur children,
  born scaly and hairy,
and clumsy on land. Their awkwardness made them angry, so they

shook their horns and gored their lovers all the way from Birmingham to Binghampton. They were loud and hobbled along on their little splayed feet, stepping on cracks on every sidewalk. Mother laid them a trail of sardines and wild game so they would not starve out there.
The children sometimes walked on glass from the time Mother was a shattered mirror
and sometimes there was ground glass in their food when they took sack lunch to school.
They walked on bloody feet and spoke with bloodied lips wherever they went.
Father thought they were awkward and quarrelsome, but Mother said they were doubly
blessed, once by Poseidon and once by Demeter, and that from their first bloody steps
and their first blood-lisped words, they were perfect.

VII.

My mother was a blue like cyanide is a blue, Prussian, evaporating. Heron, whale, mirror, gingerbread woman, riverboat, mermaid. She married my father, an ordinary swain, a swan on a lake of obsidian, a reflection in blue light with piano music, a whaler with a roulette wheel on a riverboat made of gingerbread, a beast with a horn. Together they had five red herrings, black sheep, ginger snaps, slivers of glass walking on bloody feet, slew-footed, who gored their lovers with their ghastly horns.

But blue blue blue blue Mother blew in off the Delta and blew kisses to them because they were perfect.

TORNADO PASSOVER PREP

When it would rage and groan across the plains,
sweep across Pulaski County down to the Plaquemines,
your grandma would tell the kids to stay inside—
"Lordy, it's just weatherin' out there, hon."
"It's a real toad swoggler," someone would add.
Grandpa Potter would take the platter and offer,
"Want some cathead, peckerwood? Some dead hog?"
"Sky sure's turning green enough," someone would
   observe.

You could eat cathead biscuits with bacon and preserves
and paint the sky peat-colored with your smitten eyes.
You could bring in Grandma's heirloom maters
to fry in breakfast's dead hog drippings for supper
after the flags all dropped on West Memphis dog races
and the deranged angels of the interstate stalk and stoop
to kiss the trailer parks lining the overridden riverbanks
and now hover over the doors of the South's very poor.
We say grace over our biscuits and maters and fry up more.

CORA C.'s LIST OF THINGS I'VE DONE:

Driven Jesus Christ to drink
Driven her out of her simple mind
Made her lose her religion
Annoyed the excuse-my-French tarnation out of her
Fit her to be tied and then some
Rolled my stupid eyes in my stupid head
Been just a fart in a whirlwind
Stomped on her last but very last nerve
Been a crow walking across her grave.

AMBITION

There are better things to be than trapped in an ER by
 tubes and wires and adjacent PCP smokers.
I could be a manically waving strip-mall inflatable telling
people to pay their taxes or buy tires
that may be destined for their blaze of glory in an Alabama
tire fire. I could be a stained-glass narthex
hugging my faithful phalanx of church ladies bearing
marshmallow gelatin salads and melon balls.

I could be your titillated old Dad in his lounger, reading
Mom's Anais Nin with curled toes in sock feet.
I could be the stringer of lights in a yard in on a Montgomery
 corner lot bellowing to one and all
"Merry Christmas from the Goldsteins." I could be a good-
sport Goldstein tapping out my Morse Code
in bulbs in the shape of a sleigh transforming a chain-link
fence into an ecumenical handshake.

I could be the chain-link fence topped by decorative razors that
"three strikes, you're out" prisoners scale,
commuting my sentence to time served. I could be a goldmine of
grievance, a Gold Rush to judgment.
I could be a nasty genital rash scrambling up the thigh of some
even nastier river-living trailer trash.
(Yes, we rumble our iron jaws and talk like the Klan anthropologist
where I'm from, leering from 4x4s.)

I could be the world's dirtiest limerick strummed by every hick
from Appalachia to Apalachicola.
I could be a duodecahedron aquarium with the world's largest
bottom-feeder grubbing my gravel.

I could be an empty cart clattering in the grocer's lot, not stopping
at yellow lines, a noisy, free dazzle
of annoyance—whee! I interrupt your day to make you listen to
empty, pointlessly chattering old me.

I could be the surging heartbeat of the ocean that I heard once
listening to my own cold ultrasound.
I could have mothered twins named Coreopsis and Thanatopsis,
who would be such well-rounded prodigies
that they could use "diaphanous" and "discursive" in long-
suffering Faulknerian cadences
that would drool so trippingly from the tongue that their words
would race with fice and tree squirrels.

I could be that final fly harassing Miz Emily's deathbed or the
mermaids' breath on Procrustes' pillow.
I could be the family member who writes your obituary that
makes you seem like a perpetually floating
turd in Grandmother's good leaded glass punch bowl. I could be
Elmer Gantry's guru on Easter Day.
I could be that stick of gum that melted into your luxury car's
leather seats that no one scrapes off.

There are better things to be than a prisoner in the ER under the
guard of TV re-runs and tubes.

SUMMER RITES IN BAL HARBOR ESTATES

We were the tribe of the Common White Children of the cul-de-
sac.
We all were cruel little Descartes, trapping worms on sidewalks
and frying them in the sun under dollar-store magnifying glasses.

At nighttime we pulled the belly-jackets off fireflies and wore
them
as navel rings. Sometimes we went to creeks and pulled the claws
off
crawdaddies, which we dried and turned into voodoo necklaces to
wear
while composing Caucasian occult verses we ritualized in
basements.
"Light as a feather, stiff as a board," was our tribe's regular
mantra.

Our rites of passage were myriad and sometimes harrowing,
even almost producing accidental double-dare scarification.
I led us in recitations inspired by the great chieftain Wallace
Stevens:
"Chieftain iffucan of Ascan in caftan, tan with the henna hackles
halt!"
and drilled them to the beat of "Abou Ben Adhem, may his tribe
increase,"
the benediction of our sacred pasty-white medicine man, Leigh
Hunt.

We scaled an eight-foot chainlink fence with barbed knots on top
to steal crabapples dangling beneath the "No Trespassing" signs.
The apples were sour and made us sick so we tested our wobbly
cypress knees of courage
by declaring through decree of Chieftain Iffucan many crabapple-

eating contests.

We christened the property Orchard Knob and played Civil War
   strategic retreat
there, but we tired of that game and invented a form of dodgeball
   played with
bricks. The rule was you had to hit below the cypress knee of
   courage but one

of the more attentive moms got upset anyway, and the cul-de-sac
   fell silent
until frayed housewives gave in and turned us out again. Then the
   Yankee
Fentresses moved in, and we welcomed them because there were
   six of them.

That meant fresh bodies for games but we would never have been
   allowed to dinner
at their house because they were Catholic and that meant they
   said grace wrong.
The Fentresses had a fig bush in their yard where fifth-grade girls
   sneaked
to play Truth or Dare with eighth-grade boys. They had a crawl
   space where the Fentress
girls played doctor democratically while Mrs. Fentress got her hair
   and nails done.

With the fresh Fentresses we'd gather on the hilltop for games of
   Slinging Statues, which
we called Flying Fentresses and sometimes Flying Buttresses,
   crushing two children's
rhymes together for pre-game chants: *Rikki tikki tembo no sa
rembo chari bari ruchi
PIP peri pembo* and *Chieftain Iffucan of Ascan in caftan,*

34

mixing this as though our teeth

were mortars and our tongues pestles. Mighty potions, the
  alchemy of our sweat,
spit, and blood. A triple-dawg dare could never be refused and
  honor retained,
so I raced all the boys on my skateboard down a long, steep
  driveway that ended
just by the Orchard Knob fence. My board was faster because its
  wheels had been

worn to flint, and it sparked with slick speed. Wayne Ashby was
  the last boy to beat,
and I raced him down the skinny asphalt driveway of Orchard
  Knob's keeper and crashed
into the Deuce and a Quarter he'd parked there because he hated
  our heathen tribe.

I broke my arm, and a Fentress girl rushed up the hill to my
  parents' door, came back
with word from them: "They said to tell you that'll teach you and
  serves you right."
Sobbing, my dangling arm fighting for attention with my bloodied
  knees and mouth,
I let the graven image-slinging, chanting, apple-thieving, doctor-
  playing Yankee
Catholic kids pray over me a strange and intoxicating healing
  chant:

Rikki tikki tembo no sa rembo chari bari ruchi PIP bari pembo.

35

CLARA'S BLADE

Clara, to hear folks tell it, was Dad's Tuesday girl;
we just thought she was the maid.
If looks could kill her eyes were straight razors.
When she was mad in bars, she'd say
"Ride my blade!" and gulp a chaser.
She buzz-sawed her way through life
and everyone else swept her dust away.
She clipped an enemies list to a pink hair bow
and, like Virginia Durr's dabbed lipstick
at a HUAC hearing, in a single stroke, blew
the lacquered kiss of death at folk.

SHELF LIFE

We all started out with such shiny yearbook promise.
Dangling by heels from loblolly, all were the Class Prophet.
Then year by year, a life strip-mined, whittled to coal dust,
the stacked tarot deck always dealing the Upside Down
 Man.

There was a girl once, in eighth grade, with eyes like
the static but awed textbook photos of Anne Frank, shining
brown marbles that too much tossing had rubbed to sepia matte.
The girl had one eye a little stray, chasing dust motes in the air.

Her face somehow had always the filthy trace of a smudged
Fudgecicle, but her clothes were pressed even down to the back
bow on her dress. She did her best with a hank of hair she set
back like curtilage with a tiny plastic pink barrette. I had seen
her duck around corners and peer back around when I passed.

She always kept to herself but that fall day, trembly as
a bottlebrush tree, she came to ask me, skittishly, would I sit
with her at lunch. She was a free lunch kid—a special line
let you know that. I was one of those shapeshifters passing time
among the socies, the smokers, the freaks, the bright-normals.

My socie friends would not have sat with her unless the Sunday
sermon told them to or they needed her to prop an honors essay.
I knew this. The girl knew this. She knew I was a permeable seam.

In eighth grade, we all gave prized people our school pictures,
jockeying for theirs like baseball cards. The girl everyone called
"Country" asked at lunch for one of mine. I had given them all
but promised I would give her my wish-box one next study hall.

That afternoon her outcast brother chambered a round that
wound up in the vault of her skull. Cops said he called her uppity.

Now you look at me as though I still exist, but I left you before I
knew you. I left you for a stray-eyed college woman in 1979.
I left you for a woman with a $500 Italian briefcase in 1997 who
wanted me for the centerpiece among her table's shiny objects.
I left you for a woman with the panicked stray eye of the hunted,

chasing a picture, evaporating into coal dust, ash, a bullet's bore.

PRIEST-PENITENT BOB

I.
I am the universal Clemenceau, and you
are my confessional business.
I'll make a deal with you, being superstitious.
You can draw the tarot of my being if
you never give me knives at Christmas.

II.
He rode with the Klan, you know.
It was just his pathetic echo of jelly
bean jars he counted as the registrar
of votes of them that ain't ours,
in another shitty 'Bama mini-city
where we stable our prize lunatics.
Always and ever earnest, he told you:
"If they can't count jellybeans, why let
them jellybeans vote anyhow?
We never rode against them unless
they wouldn't take care of their families.
Take care of your family." That
patriarch, stupid and stubborn
as God's last mule, ran a gas station and
gambling hall, a locus of ridicule because
Baptists shouldn't have pool tables.
(They never took their cues to church.)
Once, my deepwater grandmother,
she of the hickory switch you picked
yourself, making punishments worse
because they were yours, then,
pain of your own choosing, womped
him upside the head for flirting
with a fire-haired girl at his pump.

I liked grandmother, for that and maybe
other things (not the switchings).
She taught me this, a good lesson:
Don't flirt with other girls at your pump.
Be serious and sober. If she asks you,
your intentions are noble. Own your switch.
My mother piled on: Don't sleep with strange
men. Men like your father's daddy are
just strange. I listened, so I never
took up with strange men. But I digress.
My other grandpa used bad words
rolling from his mouth as slowly as
home-rolled tobacco (he wondered
where his rolling papers went
whenever the grandkids came to visit),
and we drove him to Sand Mountain for
either sorghum or salvation. I can't
place it now. Seems too late to recall.

III.
You may wonder why this all comes up,
sitting on a barstool in St. Louis.
I have a friend whose grandpa was named
Bob, like a stitch, a palindrome, and
he repeated through kin, like a thread, or
a moniker he never gave himself. I
didn't know him, this ordinary Bob
who was a church elder by some lights
and an atheist by others' but when I
came to Grandpa Bob's funeral
(never having much known my own,
or anyone else's grandpa), I thought that
this might just be a man who would grin
at his funeral, and laugh to see

what I saw at the Schnuck's today.
The grocery put Thucydides' quotes
on a box of fortified Tasty-O's.
You heard me right, a cereal box.
You heard me, right? My wife's
a Classics major, so we laughed
and laughed about Thucydides
of the cereal box, after Bob's interment.
They meant it for a kid's game—on the
cereal box, I mean—not Bob's burial,
because Schnuck's grocery didn't
know Bob. But cereal's no laughing matter.
Laughter's no kid's game, either, Bob.

IV.
My father sat in his recliner, working
crossword puzzles with short words
like "sward." I watch my wife work
woo-hoo fangalutin *Times* cross
words, drawing her swards sheath-
like around her, a self-caress, shielding
Innisfree of solitude, of self. Dad's
Ray Charles croons in my head. "Release
me, my darling . . . Can't you see you'd
be a fool to cling to me. So release me
my darling, let me go." Raylettes fade as
she nuzzles her own Dad's image in his
Barcalounger and mouths this puzzle, the
Miracle fabric of the '60s, "Herculon?"
Too obtuse for puzzles, I ask her:
"What is a sward?" Too abstruse for
fables, this keeper of minor arcana,
queen of hearth and home, says,
curtly and precisely, "A green lawnlike area."

That's not what I was looking for, so
I persist. Her hand-flick: move on.
Demurrer, a word only
lawyers know, at all our cross-
clued across and down addresses.
She knows what a rill is, not for
protecting the waters of this earth
she's sworn to, but instead for use in hymns
hummed behind black curtains
in your white patent-leather shoes.

V.
The ties that bind, strangle or
Bungee-cord-propel us into life,
spring us back to where we've been,
a miracle fabric of psychedelic
conundrums, Bob. Conundrums,
like palindromes, or the little
mousy hickory-dickories that metronome
our blood. "Want to cut the cord?"
the doctor asked, when the child was born.
"No," I said. "Never. This one thing
will tether, anchor, weigh me always."
I would not cut sorghum in January
or interrupt the hypnotic suggestions of
ancestors, or pretend to Sand Mountain,
or slice cords as fine as angel hair to
string us up and along like a box kite,
carrying our sensored prayers with them.
When my only child was born I knew
then that we are insulated only by air
and the arrogance of self-replication.
I knew then that love at best exists
defiant of mirrors that want only

in dimmest lighting to reflect our acts.
Did you have this reflection, too, Bob?

VII.
I have a Platonic universe of them,
and maybe a grandpa named Bob.
I have captured my wife at Sand Mountain
or at the Current and Five Forks Devil's Den,
or scaling the Duomo to avert my descent
to Hell. Her house keys are splayed on
the tabletop like a floral spray at
every funeral for every Bob, a compass
for errant fools like me. I have her in a poem
I claim is only about a sad tall oak
whispering its leaves to dirt and tell her
that rustling is not saying her name.
There, unyielding, huge, pinnate
palm of creation's subterfuge—I tried,
Bob, to stop it, but it came, and all,
all and under, the story's the same:
Family tree from Eden's roots, shading
the blazing grass. If I repeat myself,
it would not be to hear myself back
through a well. If I lie, I will lie about poems
and alms and churches and sometimes
about trees flaming in absent gardens.

VIII.
See, it's just as I told you.
An uncle will out an atheist
at his presbytery, for the sake
of the honesty of all hymns,
for all leaves falling from your family tree.
Trees tell the truth, from roots to

shedding. They shield the fragile
grass on which we walk and give
us that one last shadow, our final shade.
My wife asked me about palm-reading,
and I referred her to the palm trees
of her youth. The life-line, she
pressed. "Not long enough. But then. . ."
I thought you knew these things, she said.
Better for us both I don't, I said.
Still, I thought you knew, she said, again.

IX.
If writing poems in church is rude
I don't know why God put golf-tee
pencils in pews and killed people
named Bob. Bob was not a
liar or a cheat. Bob was just the
sort of guy you'd want to meet.
He wasn't some drunk steering
the Titanic into a gigantic
iceberg. At worst, he was
an atheist in church. Bob
was a sober lookout peering
stern to portal but never wondered
about soft horizons, or too many
stars, or earthing us with
familial swards or sundering us
with Eden's one sword, or
doubting love. Bob was a
steady captain, a straightforward
stay-the-course sort. He knew
that love lying ahead subjects us
to the tyranny of cereal boxes veering onto
your breakfast counter, strewing crumbs.

X.
Bob, I hate living with people.
Every year is an awkwardly eliding
plane, colliding still like Abel and Cain, and
between you and me, Bob, people you love
steal your hats, your time, your gloves.
They take your memories and then call
them theirs. They stomp on your nerves,
Bob, and on your stairs. Then they tread
soft on your heart and whisper, "Ours."
That's what breaks you, Bob, this
knowing that they will arrange all the
deck chairs on your ship, and hum
"Nearer my God to Thee" at the
funeral of any passing atheist.
These are the people who leave
sponges in your sink, who have the happy
stink of love about them, who
untidy your flood compartments and
accidentally break your things, Bob.
You don't know how lucky you are, Bob,
to be rid of these demanding stowaways,
genetically imparted double-helixes of love
creeping up on us in our prayer closets.

XI.
I had a dream, Bob. My brother and my
wife's sister were driving my car. You and
I, Bob, take the keys and compasses
because we saw through the mirage, Bob,
and past the horizon deceiving us with
stars tarrying like brooding overlords.
I believe you would understand, Bob.

My wife dreamed, at the same time, of an
airport, because she flies in her sleep.
I can smell her wings when she breathes.
I don't know what near-misses she has
with frozen mirages in her sleep,
what catastrophes she averts.
In that sacred portal, Bob, I
never see her. I wonder, did you see
your wife in dreams? I'd trade dreams
with her, because driving makes me mad,
Bob. In my dream my sister-in-law
Is cussing the traffic like I do. Did you
cuss at the wheel, Bob? Dreaming, I
roll in slumber and mumble to my wife,
"You have a type. It fits you like a glove."
"Yes," she says, floating in rivulets
of her inviolable sleep. This
is the dream, Bob, you and I keep,
of navigating Labrador currents,
even cussing the stars from the helm.
Let the flying spirits weep while you and I,
Bob, dream of all things unburnable,
unquenchable, unsinkable,
perilously invisible in the dark-deep.

YOUR OBITUARY SAID YOU WERE DEAD

I did not write it, having known an able actress of 22
in a time of moonstruck ambiguity when everyone
22 was a starry-eyed prophet, and actress, too.

It said you died unexpectedly, a code perhaps for
what the psychiatrist once said: emotionally labile.
He meant you were neither all fragile nor wholly stable.

If I wrote your obituary, it would have said you lived
unexpectedly and expectantly, eying your next betrayal
so that no one beat you to it this time, this one last time.

If I wrote it, it would be an advice column, a pablum,
telling us to unstudy indecision, be done with the thing.
If I wrote it, it would ring with the poetry of daily murders.

It would curdle tears to icicles for later use, a gloss
for martinis, clinking the lecture that all losses, all losses
ring in conjecture, and echo, echo just past us in passing us.

KEEPING TIME

You can call this a poem against resentment
or an appraisal checking the exchange rate of sentiment.
In Montgomery, the land the New South forgot,
we were shown a house where every brick, even
the chimney, was a cool cotton-candy pink. It
teetered there on the brink of aesthetic
extinction like an estuary for the Sisters Grimm.
It was, instead, the blue house that we bought.
Either might have felt like home to you, these
Disneyworld pastels, Floridian pustules.

I hated the blue house's hearth tiles
so I crowbarred them, and the rosewood clock
started running again, and began to chime
right around Christmastime. That old
Victorian clock has laid down its judgment
of time in five houses since, most sold to us
in divorces, and sometimes, unwound
I think I hear it ticking along, a breath,
keeping time with every place we've kept.

LONG DIVISION

A house divided by silence, they tell you, cannot stand,
but it has bricks and mortar enough, rattling sounds and
distorted hisses of boilers under those rotting eaves.
It's landlocked, hemmed in by light-blocking neighbors
crammed so tight one whole side abjures windows.
You can plant caladiums by your dreary basement,
about all that thrives in the weary Chicago sediment.
It stands up well enough, is a tough old broad hauled
all the way to Oak Park on the backs of draft horses after
it outbreathed the tumult of limestone facades burping cinders
kicked up by Mrs. O'Leary's maligned old heifer.

It must have been cabled to a dray on Austin or Division.
It doesn't belong here, its egg-and-dart and bullseye,
makeshift Eastlake with a faint whiff of smoke I smell
when it likes a new paint, a fresh burnt offering to
the god of fire who spit it out in 1873. I
make these improvements to sell it, and this house
rewards me because it likes that I am leaving it:
rewards me with smoke for the choices I made.

Its roof is the most steeply pitched in the whole town,
and it knows it, knows it doesn't want its lot, sneers
at the bungalows all up and down the avenues.
It doesn't know its place, or recalls its place too well.
The roof quarrels with the basement's worst fears:
new baseboard heat of which the smoke does not approve,
dragging the sound reproof of unvapored silence.

I remember another steeply pitched roof, another house,
lavish in its aloneness, greedy in its sashweight windows.
A careless party guest, not knowing cats seek heights,

let her out. You barely knew me then, hardly knew yourself,
but cat-coaxing, you clung to the chimney. Years later I
asked you why you clambered up on that roof, made a
Tennessee Williams joke in that Indian Summer heat.
"I thought you could use some help." Roof, cat, you,
a puff of smoke from the grill—clinging to a chimney
that sometimes flung bricks from a great height—
unexpected help. This is standing well enough.

A REBEL YELL ON MICHIGAN AVENUE

Corsets of snow belly-bust traffic in Chicago,
mercifully blurring the blocky derangements
of Mies van der Rohe's window arrangements.
You look from Floor 23 down at Michigan Avenue,
wax maudlin for a platter of deep-fried kudzu.

We are not meant for such a graceless place,
its buildings faceless, its rapacious bland spaces,
its huge inhabitants, its malignant tenements,
its grim aborted experiments with Southside facelifts.

We were invented for the Redneck Riviera,
the eternal Virginia Reel with Miz Scarlett O'Hara
ravishing her radish from the ruined ramparts of Tara.
The fantasy of Atticus Finch has leeched into our marrow.
The world is too wide for us, and we are far too narrow.

You curse at the grizzled face of an October blizzard,
rooting furtively in your desk drawer for your scissors
as though you could cut out this gray lake-effect misery.
You remember a Gulf summer storm raining mystery
in its suddenness and intensity, a Pass Christian* secret
 story.

Just like your Dad, a sharecropper's son, thrust his fist
through the sky, through Mrs. O'Hara's portieres, trusting
against evidence that there are no ghouls in Clark Gable's mist,
and reached past cotton fields, reached North, wrist-slitting,
insisting to Dixie, "Lord, there's something better than this."

---

* Pass Christian is pronounced "Pass Chris-tee-YAN."

JENNY FROM MONTGOMERY

The semi-permeable membrane of memory
today gives you Jenny of the pennies
in Montgomery's second-skin hazy heat,
Jenny in her black skirt and gauzy black blouse
at the bus stop where bluebloods' maids
in 1950s Cloverdale wilted and waited,
not too far from the Pickadilly meat-and-three.
"Do you have some pennies?" she'd say
every day to the Yankee and Yalie law clerks
come to deliver our sad Southern selves
from the wretched remnants of tattered
Stars and Bars history and peanut butter
enunciation, our finest barristers to them
as quaint as Jenny, whispering judgments
in their smug asides, visiting our lives like
a plague of poison Ivy League anthropologists.

She couldn't have liked these rich
mannerless brats any better than I did, outside
the courthouse prospecting for pennies.
"I do collect them, you know." A Yalie
who once fingered my blouse to assure
herself it was real silk and called my first
house by Bellinger School a shotgun
shack tried to give her a dollar. She drew
a Titan's armor around herself
when she pulled that gauzy blouse taut,
straight-shouldered. "No charity,
just pennies for my collection."

Now, grown and chewing on the long bones
of the law, when I see pennies I see property,

I see the pain of easements and pennies as
the easement of pain. Abolish these petty
appeasements to the god called Caesar!
He's a wastrel in receivership.
I would rather give to Jenny's collection.
Pennies, for the keeping, are safer there.

LIVE FAST OR DIE (Partlow, a Segregated Facility for "Mental Defectives")

This is a perpetual mourning
poem. If you were told to live
fast, you'll be aghast at life's stretch,
a thing too long for haiku, since
elegies have length, and heft, or maybe
fool that you are, you don't know
you can't write your own, and they'll
kill you if you can't live fast. They'll
kill you if you want much, too, if
you want more than gravel to chew,
and they'll kill you if you want to, but just
can't. This law of Nature--man's too,
rewards malignant neglect until
we can forget your forms, your faces
pleading your humanity with sallow eyes.

She's red in tooth and claw, they'll
say, as if you'd know between the two laws
which one they meant. We make places like this
for the ones with brains passing too slow
into our fast lane, or veering across lines
we've drawn for polite traffic at a pace
without speed bumps, crosswalks, not for we
who go fearlessly and live fast. If you know
all this, you know the pressuring presence
of unmarked tombs on the premises. Peace is
easily borne for the slow-footed, slow-witted.

Yet you know nothing, slumbering, clambering
like any child from the womb. But know this:
You mother stored you there like all these

discontented relics and specimen jars you can't
understand—never could—her dearest suffering,
you child of hers, child of God (Nature's too),
prisoner of all social traffic laws, no one's
parlor talk. They'll kill you slow and say
you're malingering. They'll kill you, they'll kill you.
They'll kill you if you can't at the least,
for once, at last! Just once, live fast.

BRYCE

What room shall we pick for Mother, Father?
All the walls are cinder-block, powder-color
of Easter egg green, one just like another.
I don't know how we like one over the other.

Why did he bring me here, and was it always
right here by the football stadium, in T-Town?
I remember these things: stomped caladiums
in the shade of columns, an Alabama autumn.

She'll have a nice room here at Bryce, he said.

There was a place a mile from there, Skyline Drive.
His cigarette ashes singed my fine hair
on the sidewalk, when he hugged her there,
and I was too small to push their faces together,
just tall enough to trace up to the sixth line
on the cinder blocks at Bryce, to hang in midair

between Dad's ashes and a tree on Skyline
Drive, as though I were etching myself there.
I wondered why he'd been so long inside
and left me on the sidewalk, left me behind.

Then we took Mother to her nice room at Bryce.

Dad told me we were going to Skyline Drive.
You can't remember Skyline Drive, my sister said.
I was two, but swear to you, I know I was outside.
See—my hair is still on fire from it—all red.

You cannot remember these things, she said.

I can, I said. *I can and it set my heart on fire.*
You do not possibly recall a thing about Bryce,
she said. *I do,* I said. *It made my hair go red.*
Still, you were two and can't remember, she said.

For years, they said "Bryce's," like it was a cafeteria.
They said Skyline Drive like it was a vacation home.

You can't think this ice-green grade-school block
looks anything like that, they said. But every day
in class, where teachers went out of their way
to taint me with the hereditary crazy brush,
I remembered the Bryce blocks like my alphabet,
blocks of September. School and visitor benches
to me were all the same, waiting for something.

Sometimes you have to go to Skyline Drive and wait
until they've found Mother a very nice room.

You do not remember casinos and racetracks
when he left you waiting in a cold, dark car
without a coat, the fogged windows cracked
just enough for some guy to bring you a snack
of French fries. You thought this is how things are.

You started to think too much, remember way
too much, so when you tried to talk one night
in some fleabag dive after he lost the dog races,
he begged that he was old and that he just might
die of exhaustion if you kept on, or a heart attack,
and if he died, you'd have to go to "The Place."

You shut up because you knew they'd tell you
There is no Skyline Drive, there is no lime wall,

57

there are no long benches except at church—
Look, you're alive, let's not beat a dead horse, y'all.
Talk like that and you'll go to a nice room at Bryce.
They'll put him in a hearse and take you to The Place.

I remember, I remember, and it makes me more
impermeable than lime walls, more dangerous
than a hairpin turn, ominous as Dad's roll of the dice,
more furious than Southern squalls, as nasty and
stray as an ash that likely foretold my birth from
some Skyline visit. Dad bet the house I couldn't recall.
He forgot: a gambler always overstates his worth.

I remember Dad, rolling everyone like they were dice.
I remember, but I don't think of him twice. My thoughts
are with Mother in Fall, shut up in her nice room at Bryce.

ROLL TIDE

Roll Tide, your Pettus Bridge
crimson with Sunday blood
but no communion.
Blood of fathers brooding
on the banks of the Alabama
where three little pigs tried
to ramma jamma yellahamma
their way out of the Union.

> *I have Troopers, said the first.*
> *I have clubs, said the second.*
> *I have gas, said the third.*

But this bridge did not burn
whatever the yearning in the
bellies of those beasts. It held
its steel. When they marched
there some were felled, parched
for the cooling waters below
them, rolling tide of justice,
fountains without whites-only signs.
The pigs bellowed in the pines.

> *Wallace cinched his belt.*
> *The sheriff wrenched his whips.*
> *Shelton clinched his noose.*

Still they did not flinch an inch.
As the stench of gas rained down
like righteous fire,
grim refiner's pyre
of blood, crimson blood,

blood all as black and white
as a houndstooth hat,
all red now, crimson, bleeding,
ebbed, flowed the pulse of centuries.
History, silent, stood,
then jumped from the bridge
down to those waters, baptized
in fire, capsized in flood
like the first brickbat
God hurled at His New World.
All this red now, bone unbreeding.

> *You didn't have to march.*
> *You didn't have to dream*
> *of any prophet's mighty stream.*
> *You just had to be black*
> *for the Black Belt and*
> *Wallace's belt to lick you*
> *and the sheriff's belt to whip you*
> *and the tear gas to kick you*
> *back as hard as any firehose.*
> *They beat four-year-olds at church,*
> *who only stood to watch.*
> *You didn't have to want justice*
> *to get it carved out rough—*
> *just being black enough,*
> *was enough.*

That Sabbath passed, John Lewis' head
split like watermelon and ABC
News interrupted its coverage of
"The Judgment at Nuremburg"
to show us rough justice, rough
rough justice meted by men tough

enough to hide under hoods
by night, tough enough to beat girls
and bomb them while they set their curls.
Nebraskans thought it was fictional
spice, social commentary,
license to splice some allegory
into Europe's remembered purgatory.
Fooled once by "War of the Worlds,"
Nebraskans would not be fooled twice.
It was only television unfurled
by some heavy-handed hacks.
This must be the war of another world.

Every man who rode against the vote,
every man who rode in the night
came home to his pure white
wife and held her tight against the dark,
telling her that Cain's tetrarch
of Wallace, Connor, and Shelton marked
his path through the arc of dusk,
that it was more than just bloodlust.

> *We've done our civic duty,*
> *fairly and not cruelly.*
> *Klan justice does not swerve.*
> *They only get what they deserve.*

General Pettus of the Late Lost Cause,
your bridge gnaws at us, whipsaws
us all in the night, in the small
pause between nightfall and just-sleep
when the creeping junk cars ride
that tide of crimson, when
the sheriff's cruisers glide the kudzu

and there is blood on the maws
of God knows all our Southern laws.

Wallace asked how long?
Sheriff said not long.
Shelton said not long.

Poor, broken Nothingcrats
slaves to the steel mills
and the Appalachian foothills.
Your fathers trudged this way
gray from pellagra.

There is a chariot but it's not here.
There is a charnel wheel just there.
There is a rough, notched rope
hanging as high or low as all our hopes
for ourselves. The air cracks
over the railing of the Lorraine Motel.

The earth and heaven save jots
and tittles, free and enslave,
until all law is, as willed,
fulfilled. When this world is your home,
say Amen. When you own this sin,
say Amen. Bleed deep crimson
with all deliberate speed.
And roll, roll, roll, tide, roll.
You're the canvas stretched against our soul.

CHARITY, TRUE CHRISTIAN CHARITY

We took in two old dogs after our pitbull died.
We took them in old because their daddy had died.
The 10-year-old hound put his heart and his head
in my hands, flagged me with a paw, and cried, cried.
He knew he was here because his daddy had died.

His sister's more game, gets in a bow-legged stance
to play dance, prances up when her name's said.
Your been-here-first dog, though, she snubs her bowl,
and your calls to her fall about as leavened as lead.
She stakes out the pit's forlorn space on the bed.

You remember, strangely, that once a step-cousin
got taken in when her daddy died and even your new
stepmother said they were trash, always rushing
state lines for debts, and your own schizo mother
said: Driftwood and beggars. They spread like rash.

Your mother, in a rare paroxysm of lucidity,
had just enough left of cultural or moral acuity
to tell you that "good people" don't call their sisters'
kids trash. She told you without ambiguity
she'll do it to you, just wait and see. Oh yessiree, mister.

I snubbed the not-my-real cousin of whispers
who took up a tight maternal pity spot I never got
even to visit, the one my shunned mother called a bitch,
that one who treated me with the silence of Vespers
when I was all of six. Cousin got the bed. I got a cot.

She said to me, I hope one day your daddy dies
and you have nowhere to go. At 40, I stood at his grave

63

and thought, right back to you. Now you know.
"Promised he'd never leave me." She grabbed me and cried.
Fitting for her, the last thing he did was, he lied.

To back-clap myself, one time I did this one small thing
that a physician or Carrie Nation or your garden-variety
policeman would have forbidden: a park-bench drunk,
same age as my dad was then, begged for money or whiskey.
It was snowing, I had piety to share, and he was thirsty.

DEATH OF A NEIGHBOR

Old Mr. Soderdahl, he outlived them all,
saw more jiltings than Granny Weatherall
among these carefully tended blocks,
his house painted in Quetzlcoatl colors
that dazzled me a little more than the others.

Still he subsisted to me in across-the-street fashion,
whatever passion spilled on the suit his dandy house
wore to look out at the more subdued places,
their two-hued paintjobs curtly unadventurous.
The old Swede's heart may have been tremulous,
but he had strength enough for all the teals
and gaudy heliotropes dripping from his brushes.

His heart, weathered though it was, may
have beat for the hot shades on his porch,
shaming the bright hummingbirds perching
there, garishly, noisily beautiful, but like
the old man himself, so slight no one heard.

NAZARETH

The woman who lived upstairs had soft red hair,
soft in tone and soft to the touch. She mistook me
for a dancer, but I was only a delicate acanthus stalk
pretending to blossom a shape, a puny, unkempt reed.
That 1860s townhouse was behind the Hawk 'n Dove.

She had a German short-haired pointer called Deli Dog
and I had six cats who moved in somewhat like Carl
Sandburg's fog had and just never dispelled to light. She
owned a shop of antiquarian books in Baltimore that
she may even have playfully named Nevermore. Every
night I would hear her hands flattering the ivory keys
just as they had taught her at Julliard, hear her playing

Rachmaninoff, Mussorgsky, almost feel her swaying
upstairs when she made for me mixtapes she left on
the landing, and I could see her sometimes standing
on those stairs, where she was humming Ray Charles,
the snarling Elvis' songs that no one knows like "Marie's
the Name (of His Latest Flame)," all of Jeannie C. Riley's
B sides. She taped for me the many versions of "Promenade
In Green" she knew, and when I heard her soft tread sneaking
away after leaving treasure, her feet on the stairs a musical
measure, I would dance to find it at my doorstep, humming

"When I go by Baltimore, need no carpet on my floor."
When she left, as vapors should, I wanted her to write an opera,
just for me, about what good thing could come from Nazareth.

CALLING THE ROLL

Let me be the curator on the day
In the long hot summer
When all hell breaks loose.
Someone needs to be in charge.

Ferguson! Hands up or I'll shoot.
Don't think I won't do it, either.
Charleston! Stop crying.
You put that thing down right now
Or I'll give you something to cry about.

San Bernardino, you're in time out.
Go to your mat. Baton Rouge!
Redstick—go get me your switch.
Orlando, I told you you'd get burned
If you touched that. I told you
A burned child dreads the fire.

All of you! Back up. Get down.
Show of hands. Show me your hands.
Keep everything where I can see it.
Dallas—Dallas, now what did I tell you
About parade routes and snipers?

Pay attention. Listen. Settle down,
All of you. Use your indoor voice
But use your words. You have to
Use your words. Meantime, what
We need—are you listening to me?
is a little
order
here. . .

CIVICS LESSON FROM CABLE NEWS

Oh you hair-gel boys with Pepsodent smiles
plying all your metrosexual wiles up and down I-95,
with the smooth clean nails only an accountant
could love, I have a benediction for you.
May you work midnights in the dishroom
of the Ambassador Hotel, cracking plates
with precision and may you stack shrimp forks
one against another like fey toddlers
grasping the skirts of nervous post-partum mothers.
May you find yourself stashing and furtively
stealing cracker packets to file in your smock pocket.
May the grievances of old hair-netted women
chatter around you like eternally embargoed press
releases, clog your working hours like grease in a drain.
May you be rinsed and stacked on the clattering belt
with the lipstick-rimmed martini glasses from a
rehearsal dinner the groom attended just to shoot the guests.
May you be a wishbone of contention spread out
at a luncheon for fez-fetishist Freemasons practicing pulley-bone
before they suck your marrow and pitch wadded napkins
at dumpsters, their imaginary championship goalposts.
Let them clean their plates and leave nothing undone.

The whole world's Texas: and your hair is closer than mine to God,
here on CNN. You can condescend to these redneck clods
because your life does in fact depend on it. If you erupted in full
Armani suit, it wasn't from the head of Zeus. You weren't
the head god's wink of an Illuminati eye. My guess is he blinked
 you
awake straight out of his opioid sleeps in Hades. Trust me:
I'm a lawyer. I stitch problems like fine embroidery, then I
iron them stiff as grandma's doily. For forensic purposes, I'm

measuring
the oxygen evacuating studio rooms, the balloons of our civic
 hope
giving up gas, farting around the place making blathering sounds,
 wafting
your narcissistic perfume whenever those rubbery lips move.

DORIAN GRAY HAS A FACEBOOK PAGE

"The Beast" knows just what I'd like for dinner,
knows what I like in my shimmering politics,
knows to send me stray benighted puppies with stitches
and a few homeless addicts on crutches
and to break the gloom, some Bette Davis, too.

666-ish, it marks my charities and the barbarities
of toothbrush-less kids in my country's cages
and it sends me strange symbols from wars long over
hovering in my news feed side bar, about a new battle
raging in Charlottesville flying antique flags, the flags
of some very bad people and some very good ones, too,
their soldiers bivouacking under tin-underskinned but
bronze-cladded equestrian statues, easily dragged down
when dark falls in the city parks. And after velvet dark

falls on the Facebook page, our collective Narcissism
rallies, calling the troops back to their own tumbling tubes
of memory, dinners, donkeys and elephants and poor beasts
brutalized by some very good people who have new tires on
their cars and mow their grass before it draws garter snakes and
recite the same prayer every day over predictable plates.

Facebook knows. Facebook knows that we all are Lieutenant
Calley, all a bit of the Sonderkommando, a fragment
of Robespierre. It sends us battered puppies to cluck over to
reassure us of our lack of complicity in some crimes, so we know
that we can't be all that manunkind, our pitiful and too-maligned
little race. Mainly it knows that we all are addicted to ourselves,
the most potent stimulant on our atomistic planets, stranded
with our "friends" and between all of us not one dose of Narcan.

O Facebook, we write on your perpetual surface what flatters us to believe about ourselves, we who are not crutch-kickers and puppy-killers, our One Vision that shatters the mirror we turn backwards on the shelf so that we can evade a representational portrait. We embrace instead your constructed mighty micro-glass of self.

A MOST IMPORTANT MAN

You think you don't know me, but you do.
I am Eliot's snickering eternal footman,
the Anti-Christ's Groom of the Stool.
My job lacks the refinement of a cabinet post,
but most of the time it has its perks. I know all
the murky details, and I have all the skeleton keys
to all the closets, and every one of them works.

You can find me at the bar, wearing my club jacket,
and I never drink alone. I'm the freaking Al Capone
in charge of investigating the misdeeds of myself.
I give a sweet caress to the hyoid bone of Elliott Ness.
I used to dine with Jeff Epstein and still spit-shine
frumpy old Billy Barr's valise and sole-less Weejuns.

Sometimes I break out the Ouija board to chat up
Mussolini, and sometimes, over a very dry martini,
we toast Mother Pence and break a crostini into
communion-size bits in remembrance of Scalia. Sure,
I aspire to the cosmopolitan pages of Esquire, like
Beto, but wind up in The Inquirer instead. Alas, alak!
Poor Yorick. I'll go to my squeaky Procrustean bed
with tee-time with the Taliban dancing in my head.

A man in my position might be called a martinet,
but I assure you, I am held in high trust, guarding
both the scepter and the flashy family jewels, rooting
through the waste, hurling prophets from the parapets.
A man in my position, a penny in the pocket of the throne,
sees the carefully choreographed musical chairs here, all
serving at the ruling sovereign's whim or as we say, pleasure,
arranging themselves in mad shapes to escape the jesters'

bullets enacted daily in the Star Chamber where the curtain falls
and they scamper and scurry into their hidey-holes in the wall.
You don't know me, but I pay the hush money and the blood
 money
to the laundress removing stains from the Emperor's new clothes.

TALK RADIO VISITS THE DISCOUNT STORE

Poor people are just like us except that
they suck more, you know, littering our
highways with their clunker cars and
changing their motor oil in the public lot
of their piteous discontents.
They infest scrubbed malls, just gawking
their desire—they're undoubtedly
only there to lift purloined wares
and shove envy in the empty
wrapper to fool us paying dupes.
Just like they steal from everyone's
favorite old uncle. The poor!
They lavish clipped coupons in store
lines, and their Kool-Aid-stained children all
are louder, more nervous than mine.
They breathe the oxygen that we
could all put to better use huffing
rarefied radio ether
telling us what to do with them.
They buy the deranged week-old fruit
in "manager's special" bins and
then these broods just get sick again,
spreading it to the rest of us.
Poor people have opinions
they didn't pay one red cent for.
Well, as the saying goes, you get
what you pay for and are there not
workhouses for those sort of folks,
those others who used to wash our
clothes and now tick up items
on registers of subtle rot?
They have the gall to smile in lines

74

at their gridlock clogs of food stamps,
wafting miasma into our
hard-earned air, thankless but smiling,
these dirty change-counting others
holding up the lane for special
processing, coupons, an extra
apple running five cents over ration,
while you're trying to buy passion fruit,
this subspecies God calls brother.

MY LORD ST. LOUIS

My Lord, St. Louis, just how
did you do this? I want to
know why someone posted
about a lost turkey in, well—
it could only be the Southside
because turkeys are just on tables
out in Ladue. I wouldn't want to
be that turkey. Neither would you.

My Lord, St. Louis, here you just are,
a little planetary scar spawning the
elements, the conundrums of T.S. Eliot,
the little piteous, discontented contents
of Tennessee Williams, his blue tenements.

Oh my Lord, St. Louis, you sit on the fault
lines that may destroy us from New Madrid
to Ferguson, and still, in your World Fair's
vault, hold our sordid and buried treasures.
I think, St. Louis, you're one tough measure.

FAULT LINES

I tremble for my country, Mr. Jefferson,
when I reflect that God is just. I tremble
like the children in cold mylar blankets

that a gust of wind could blow from cages
where they sleep on cold concrete that
might just be the bedrock of our nation

I tremble, and my tremors are a terrible rage
that might shift tectonic plates on fault lines
that always were the witch at the christening

I tremble hot magma hardening to igneous

I tremble at the thoughts and prayers of
indifferent pedigree knitting a stench in the air.
And when anger hardens, it trembles no more.

ARCH CITY

St. Louis, arch-browed ironic city, you break my heart.
You're all Creve Coeur, right from the start.
Sometimes, you're all Archbishop collars, and then
You're just people begging dollars on your streets.

St. Louis, you break my heart. We just cannot, so
I will start talking to you, but you already broke my heart.
Just today, I saw a woman with an autistic son on my block.
Some good soul had given him a small chocolate milk. Maybe
it was silk for his tiny little mouth. I hope so. I hope so.

His mother, I know, had an ongoing flirtation with death.
You can call it opioids. You might pronounce it crystal meth.

She only wanted—and wouldn't you—just to feed her kid.
I saw this slow dance unfolding, and I offered her food. She
declined, but she gripped my hand. "Blessings," we said at
the same time. She said to me, "Thank you for seeing us."

I did not know whether to wash or preserve my hand, the
Stigmata of her touch. The hand of a stranger burned that much.

ST. LOUIS WINDCHIMES

When the gunshots ring out in the nighttime
instead of the church bells, we call it
St. Louis windchimes and when they do it
on Christmas, we say they're urban carols.

We sandblast graffiti because it's thug street
trash we want gone, and it stays down awhile
but the day after Christmas here in our home
on Grand by the ghetto Schnucks and the methhead
mini-mart parking lot by the Kentucky Fried Murder
franchise, a street mural in its place, in oil paints,
proclaims "This is a hostile takeover" and it is as

beautifully tendered to us as frankincense and myrrh.
We hear a voice that is not a chambered round, not
a bang, not a whimper, but just maybe a prayer
singing, wringing itself out in the streets of our city
like a crisp, clear, ring it, children! silver bell.

ON EMILY POST PROBATION IN ST. LOUIS

I am late in saying thank you to the city for the tar-filled blessings
of antediluvian potholes finally filled and smoothed with the
  roller,
for the cacophony and profusion of perpetually confused squirrels
returning the effusive embraces of oak and catalpa in the parks,
for the magnolias lining their roundabouts so improbably this far
  north
of the frost line, for the cornucopia of German stone masons and
  the
German beer barons who hired them to build their barrel-
  chested

brag-homes jutting over Mississippi River bluffs who sometimes
  shot
themselves within the gloomy walls just a quick trot from their
  taprooms,
their vistas now gravel factories and those crop-circle refinery
  canisters,
silty excavation sites, the coal-fired spire proclaiming "Excelsior"
vivisecting the sky that the Sisters of Carondelet share
  apprehensively
with them—but the brewers' names loom still over stadiums, while
Palladian windows bloom melancholy toward the curb of Lemp's
  stark house,

names tattooing brick sides of shops on Arsenal, Jefferson,
  Antiques Row—
staring over the vulgar traffic on Broadway fleeing for the Illinois
  side—
the Busches, the suicidal Lemps, Uhrigs, Wainwrights, Griesediecks
  laid
away at Bellefontaine in garish death houses built by German

stone masons
while outside the gates someone has graffitied "Welcome to St.
 Louis,
Gateway to the West, Arch City, the Republic of Red Velvet
 cupcakes."

DISCOUNT BAZAAR ST. LOUIS

At the ghetto Schnucks sometimes
you see a woman in a hijab
postering "There is no Muslim War,"
citing the Treaty of Tripoli.

Sometimes there's a little girl
in a fluffy stained pink coat twirling
away from her back-handing mama
in pajama pants, swatting and snarling.

Sometimes the slow food stamp lines
frustrate the fluctuating drunks
hopscotching from cashier to cashier,
snapping like hypertensive brassieres.

You throw parking-lot popcorn
and the pigeons storm the asphalt
for their gastronomical gestalt.
You dream a murmuration of birds

forming careful V's, swarming sunsets.

GROUNDING BY STARS

The wild alchemy of stars is all your eyes'
gleaming. We navigate this seamless wilderness
through its seeing, and pat trees' ghostly moss,
one hour's insurance on seasonal loss, a profile
tossing like any two-faced Janus in my head, tilting
like symphonic bars but never meant for hearing, grim
notes that never, never could shake you. They'll split,
these stars, knit themselves back into constellations,
as stars do. I would never wake you here because
the stars need their rest. I would tell you that sometimes
I let them spell me, ask them to visit earth, numbly alert
and dreaming, to follow your route in moonbeams, tracing
or erasing your steps past potted ferns in stale and
dusty libraries, reading your Little Golden Books on
shelves of memory that cannot forget themselves. I've seen
these lurking stars, skulking by elevators that carry us
down, pummeling us to earth ageless as gymno- and
angiosperms, sharp-toothed as dinosaurs, worthless
as the last rattling breath of a fetid pillow pleading with
the reaper for your health. Oh these nefarious stars
batter the doors of our petty scarred terra-monte, to drag us
back against time, to sputter their spent gaseous blazes
on our home hearths, and pronounce their paths to elegant
extinction, heaven. Bilious masses, they seem so neat and tidy
dressed in Orion's flashy belt. They pierce our static biology
with promise, and threat, and mortality. They call us to
the small, blessed, dream-tossed Eden of serpentine angels
sleeping prayerfully and unawares on adjacent feather pillows.
We know them only by their sleeping shapes. The stars
know them by their charted geography and dust-clouds of breath.

ATOMIC WEIGHT

The atomic particles of memory
fuse or diffuse your life, but
what is the weight of remembrance?
It can be so exact it implodes brick,
leaving buildings erect, intact
while deconstructing bone and flesh.
It can detonate from great distance.

Memory can be the moment a train comes,
with its steel-wheeled dragging integrity,
chugging its breath at your face, splitting
you for a moment between cities it visits,
the infinitives of its itineraries,
leaving you shuddering on the platform
wondering where you lost your footing,
mumbling in search of a misplaced mitten.

It jolts you forward toward the jumping off
point of the trestle and into the fissure.
The holy elements shape themselves into words
reorganizing, reconstituting all that matters.
We know its sheer destructive pressure
but can only guess the weight of its concrete shoes.

BRUMALIA

This is the place I have made,
this falling light, thin air
slivered through the blinds.
This is the hunger we create,
the wonder of all blessings
sweeping at the garret grate,
ending in melancholy
thunderclaps, a scirocco perhaps,
a frenzied, blundering dance.

This is all—those cracks in the blinds,
your house, your home, your tranced
cinema unreeling even itself, just
now, in the blighted gray light
that no prophet or seer is caressing,
a genetic curse of race memory:
a tremor in the pulse, chromosomal
celluloid recording us for dingy vaults
rebutting the insults to be dealt by time.

Take that wafer, now, and quiver.
It could be all you have, now or ever.
That and only that, a transubstantiated
savior, the dark malingering stranger
in our blood. A silent movie flickering
like this December, a slithering prayer.

HALLOWE'EN

Hang October's black wreath on the door
For the lover who will knock no more
For the partner in this danse macabre
For graves this city wind will rob.

Gossip's white sheets will flap their boast
That beyond this door lies summer's ghost.
Neighbors injudicious at the curb
Will cluck and chuckle and observe
Furtive goings-in, private comings-out
And feast on tricksters of our doubt.

But we two know all of autumn's guile
Set in the jack-o-lantern's smile.
October, love, the thing that parts
Hobgoblins of our too-small hearts.

"Love is thicker than forget"—e.e.cummings
"Objects in rear view are closer than they appear."—General
Motors

REDSHIFT

I.
If I could find a way to lie to you,
to shape my hands to scoop up such
bright and innumerable lies
as I would invent for you, I would.
In truth, I still recall you indifferently
snatching your body back into the black hole
it always was. You've owed me diffidence,
to be once more a kaleidoscope
of darkness, no more than a spent halo
in the tossed wasteland of space.
Even then I had forgotten that once
I saw you cradling in those arms
all that dignifies the night:
Glimmering origami of stars.

II.
Caroline, there was a time
when I could trace my disembodiment
on your face, in your blazing
nebulous eyes, Prussian blue as cyanide.
Must we all then weep, and you
with both eyes open now? Did I forget?
If I have forgotten you better then
to be swallowed by alienation,
captive in some yawning crater
on a cold moon spun off its axis.

Better to be radio silence, just dead air.

III.
I have unremembered you easily as life
forsakes its seed, its poor ghost driven
far beyond the idle martyrdom
of *this* kingdom. Am I then a lie?
Can I call you a lie, when in all
that is beautiful to me your face
interposes, in a glimpse I sense
as an imprinted perfume long diffused?
When in my heart still I hear
the trapped fluttering of a solitary
bird veering away like the desolate
lost lie of a prayer?

IV.
Will there be a time when fingering
my pockets for existential dimes
that I might find a yellowed movie ticket
and something in me will snap
like the thin crossed skeletons
of twigs you stacked to build a fire?
You gave no quarter to winter.
You asked me to bring you a log,
and all voices besides yours that instant
have long since dwindled to silence
like the heartbeat of a stillborn.

V.
I was afraid of you, I confess it now.
Your touch set me trembling between flesh
and hell's precipice. I thought I saw

in one swift terrible burst
the horrible push from the womb
and the hand on the hearse, and
tumbling, saw your life flashing
like a pulsar before my eyes.
"You won't write about this, will you?"
you breathed to me; I breathed back "No."
Then I wrote: Rosemary is for remembrance.

VI.
Are you a shadow lengthened by silence?
In old photos you stand just to my side,
posture casting blushes of shade.
But look! Those eyes in the dusk,
the great liquid blue eyes, peer out
all penumbra, insinuation.
They are hooded with uncertainties,
spinning off from me even in still life,
azimuth, parallax, gone.
Gone in the moment of apprehension
Gone in the moment of catch a falling
star, never to be pocketed. Spent.
But Caroline, you have something of mine
shut up like Mary in the tower.

VII.
I have forgotten what I cannot spin without.
It must be the music of all stars.
I hold your picture to the light
to grasp the last shadow-ash
in your teeming expectant eyes.
The umbral shadow on your cheeks,
Caroline, is the first vague sign
of the certain change, our apostron.

But in those blueshifting orbs
lies the locked treasure that is yours,
Caroline, and that is mine.

VIII.
I was false to call you beautiful.
If you are beautiful, Keats was mad.
Let him string gossamer filaments
star to star and be a glad fool,
keeping stupid company with me.
No, you cannot be beautiful.
Fortuitous is a better word, better
because you always have an umbrella
whether hurricane or meteor shower.
You are beautiful chiefly because
you have the sense to come in from the rain.
But all this is long forgotten now.

IX.
Funny thing, the courage lying takes.
The liar is brave enough to separate
from his heart's desire his schemes
to secure it, fondling stratagem
as much as object. Lying,
a lawyer's habit, is second nature,
and deft lying, the craft of winning.
A lie I could have told you but did not:
I swear I saw you once spinning
through the fire-ringed firmament.

X.
Poems are lies. You knew this, too—
Words in high heels, chaste seductions,
the pathos, librations. You resisted.

Still there was a time—this thing is true—
that I was an orchard in winter
glazed and bowed down with ice,
quivering, wanting a cover from you.
And here, quasar, flare star,
you dominate the infinite space
of memory. Stars are what they are.
My perch, a less lofty one. Here sings
one lost bird on a frozen branch
chattering from the bare-treed highlands,
awed by your ferocious light.
Oh Love, only truth, only Universe
I bless, I know, I hold, forgive
All strutting words, and forget, forget.

REMONSTRANCE

What is this melancholy scuttling up the stairs
toward the sepia tone of memory? You're at sea
in the Hebrides of your head, or falling gracelessly
from the cliff of mistakes you've made while trying
like Magellan to locate the exact longitude of regret.

On memory's crumbling shelf, you have only yourself
to endure, dimly conscious, fumbling. You know the whole time
that these stairs you climb to the ill-lit precipice
of your small ambitions, your artifice, your little life—
there will be greener graves than yours
to desecrate or to endure.

OLD LOVERS ARE FAT

Learning of lapsed lovers grown fat
on the seeds of addiction,
I congratulate myself on my prescience.
Ankles oppressing shoes, ship of thigh
bruising its mate, burdening skin.
Near-misses, half-divorces, nothing that
eats the ground glass of affliction;
the worst was no more than unpleasant.
The touching left no sign of crossing I
might mark (but they were thinner then).

I preside over my Empire of Needs
like Maslow with Mao's Five-Year Plan.
Persephone swallowed and stayed in hell.
Eve had an apple and in the tasting
lost God, found man, a sour wager.
You sigh for spring, amid winter's weeds.
If I plow this stone of a decade, can
purchase throttle barricade, quell
the knowledge that we are wasting
and the cosmos a blighted stranger?

You sigh, check the calendar for spring.
I check for reflex, chart the course,
the broken geometry of your moods,
read the bulletins of my divorces,
wondering how bloated they've grown.
Winter, here, is nothing more than a sting
in my bones—nary more. Not remorse.
Like that girl in Hades, I held on to the goods.
I congratulate myself on my choices.
Would Persephone eat a stone?

OCTOBER WALK IN TOWER GROVE PARK

I like the justcrisp letter-sweater weather of late October,
when the pale imminence of winter is barely being
bear-poked at night, still hibernating while the mums
yet bloom in their tight candy-corn clutches.

Winter will soon enough spit at us through its white teeth,
but not on a day like this, when russet petals flee the trees,
aspiring cloudward before finally despairing to mulch.
Not on this day when your shuffling, aimless feet crunch
deciduous palmate veins back into their burrows of earth.

THE ANONYMOUS LETTERS OF GLORIA VANDERBILT

At the flea market, she bought a perfectly trussed parcel
of letters and placed them, unread, in a transparent
plastic cage she keeps like a laboratory specimen
in her studio. She had bathed in the fragrance of
old onionskin and the scent of lovers' touches on
the yellowed envelopes and holds them, unopened,
in trust, still binding the secrets that spill onto pages
from the heart's blood of lovers' murmuring pens.

In the graveyard of poetry anthologies, we plunder
dead scribes' rhymes with untutored reading, wondering
why the Royal Academy let Burkes and Hares like us
visit your graves, ragpick you to breathe new life into
our archives. But a few of us know that you wrote not
for us, but in defense of the sanctity of secret intent
to which we supply the content, suborning hidden
discontents. A few of us collect flint, schist, mica
or even fool's gold to pirate away your rest, leaving
one mineral kiss of emulation on your headstones.

In the end, all letters are bound with the twine and
caution tape of our lives, marking casements that
are not to be pried by voyeurs when they're left behind.
Gloria left these strangers' secrets safe in a see-through
box, mysterious even though within reach. Like the
dead poets, she shares our gift of ambivalence, knows
the worth of the underrated strategically placed footnote.

TURNING

The plaintiff in error stands at the bar.
This voice is that of trust eroding
at light-speed, one million hands
banging gavels of final decision.
These small choices of nothing much
to say, resound into dull, null days
unbreathing themselves, untether-
ing, catch us breathless, deathlike.
If I must not be me then surely you
can't be you, just this star-crossed
patterned tree bending to weep, asleep
in my back yard. I saw it, bowed.
We (,), like leaves (,) or judgment
falling, swirl separate, apart. Distant
as those stars I once saw you keeping,
distaff as oars steering you wrongwise,
each stroke of your slaveship yoke.

Rivers whirl like leaves between us.

These currents foreign seas, churning--
and I'd run these long ceaseless
lines, I'd ride this reckless, feckless
tide, would make this wave a soft break.
I'd live for you in shade, would drown
the simple sun, would be done of it
and free myself—at least myself! If

I could. But I sleep, and dream of waves
crashing, and leaves, and decrees burning
up September's fire, since from that fall
no tremulous wave, no trembling leaf,
no sound of surf or silence is returning.

SUSPENSION

You'll chain me like poor Prometheus to context.
"All things being equal," you'll say, as if they
were. They wear thin, your devices, this artifice, your
pale sacrifices to form, thin as the lilypads of ice skim
ming frosted rivers, splintering the brutal, ethereal light
of winter viewed from the sad suspended height of trestles
we don't cross now. You're just a Vedic truth I keep
to myself. Pathetic, far delusions of mirrors, these sad
illusions of sameness, paralytic seams of memory.
They'll keep, all these secrets that'd be spoiled in the
telling. They'll keep until I rest, and you weep. And
you, too, will crumble and tremble into the rusted dust of
Was, *Was*, an Indian Summer wasted on the hustings.

My peripatetic eyes fool even me, pacing out mysteries.
I know little, but I do know enough of that rough and
tumble business of time demarcating your face from mine.
Within your reach, once, constellations bloomed like
bulbs, your hands ovations to all good things flowering
forth, insisting to a tired earth your own special worth.
Within your reach once, lilies stargazed the moon and
Narcissus mused a watery twin. Once. Then again

these reflecting pools will drown us. Ophelia choked on
laurels, not wafers. Better to gulp, close lips,
take—air or water, it doesn't much matter. Live, die,
float. Bloat yourself on salvation. Sit. Pray. If you want
starve. Choose. Stay! Appoint each minute of
come-what-may your muse. The catechisms of Everyday
break us down, down, down, deconstruct
our roses, turn our puny floral sprays of words
charnel, spin us funereal, mourning, churning us

back to earth, a march for a marionette we never
quite knew or rightly met. Spin these stupid poses
round and round and round until like all Edens,
every bower, we come undone, undone, undone

        undone

           entirely

                  under canopies of flowers.

VALENTINE

Deny, deny all.
Deny that the heart is deep wellshaft
blowing echoes of the music of one voice.
Deny that I am the colors under which you fly.
Deny.

Deny the body's memories,
fugues the mind blinks past.
Deny the chorus of your chanting soul.

Deny you would rather hurl yourself
from the cold impregnable parapet
than forget your name stumbling from my lips.
Deny this.

Deny that your heart foretold me
as pressure drop forecasts hurricane.
Deny that I am the shadow on your wall
throwing gauntlets to distance.
Deny, deny all.

You carved my initials into your hand
with a gaucho knife, alone on another coast
and thought of my kiss.
Deny all, but never this.

Yet despite your purgative devotions,
your erratic amygdalin emotions,
these little percussive convulsions,
it never was you that I ever loved.

I loved a gold-haired doctor but she loved

her scalpels. She said I loved my steel-cut words
better than her. Still, I'd have let her slit me bow to stern.
Even her raging blue eyes raked me like razors
as she leaned in close, whispering, "Be not afraid."

LOVE POEM

Darling, while I was gone for the summer
you heated gas on the stove and burned
down the house, and darling, while I was
gone, you invited a snake pit into the kudzu
and they strangled every last flower we had.

This is what I had heard but when I returned
the house stood true against the falling sky
but one dog was dead and another ripped
in his throat. I know my people always said
you were a little cold-natured for a Southern girl.
It must be those Yankee Calvinist parents you had.

GARDENS

And if the moon presses itself into your smile
and the cryptic hexagram of a snowflake
pronounces itself in your every gesture,
and if jazz blues brass bands shiver my veins
occasionally first seeing you of a day, what of it?
If I remark every pause, every crease
In your conversation and cerebral confetti
cloudbursts if your little voice trip-traps
some transparent guide wires in my head,
and if Mermaid and Minotaur shimmer
and glide in some shifting interior landscape,
and I watch like one tranced, then what of it?
And if some dammed-up, trapped poetic vision
suddenly like a lost metaphor wishing
to reclaim itself explodes and takes Mermaid
and seawall amid sounding of self-derision,
takes all things fallible with it, torrential,
and still I stand, lone proud spectator
to the chaos of my life cascading past,
is this a shattering that matters?

And if I have a curious, sometimes serious
Hallelujah chorus in whatever part moves
slow as the iris of your eye or beggar's purse unfolding
sometimes when you speak and fugitive eyes
avert themselves like an indecipherable
simile ineluctable on my lips
to make me die of thirst, parched, hollow—what?
What then, if I should flower and fail
and frail interrogatories beseech you from
a place far past all terrains I ever walked
and the moon catches in my smile reflecting

yours, and I accidentally bloom the secret nighttime
unrequited blossoming of the iris
of all eyes, your eyes and eyes of God's whisper,
what of this neon blitz in my head so busily
undoing me and my machinations?
If impossibility like the unreadiness of my days
collapses the negative integer I call a life
taken by antediluvian fiat, tell me by what
name I can still call you that you would hear
the slow tremor of my pulse pronouncing you
in noiseless space, without the deliberate sad
arithmetic of marking my days here.

Tell me if from the parallax of my dull
ineffectual calculus I can divine the ratio
of hunger enough to siren blood and bone, make it
sing like your most reticent voice, symphonic
on my ear, distilling itself to a point of absolute
unclarity, some advection current flowing
over us to a more uncertain destination,
unrefined, subterranean, camouflaging
fog, ephemera obscuring circumspection.
Tell me if there is a roadsign in the miasmic
fugue of our wanderings. Could I follow
my own tracks back this indifferent path now,
marking hexagram, iris, the startled shape
of my own footsteps circling in hesitation
and studying themselves at every feckless
turn, thinking oh, how these frenzied steps
incriminate me, and what if in this dense
wilderness you've been listening, watching
the eccentric progress of my groping
for a handhold in flood, forest, underworld,
sympathetic but distant as the constellations,

seeing my steps play tag in their concentrics,
what then? It is known that footprints
admit of no retraction. Even retracing
no more than subtly reconfigures, is a vain
subterfuge mocking the subterfuge of flowers,
altering just enough, halting, about-face
staccato drumming of repeated indecision.
Prometheus bound never gathered so much stone
as I gather in my little silences, valence
of bluff, innuendo, paralysis of granite.

And if I advance, seeking no permission,
thinking that somewhere under hexagrams
of frost love-lies-bleeding, irises, purple
florets will wake and a dormant world unravel,
baffling me, that a whole drowsy earth
wants the razzle-dazzle of birth out of sleep, what of it,
unless I should misstep and crush the innocent breath
of a whole regiment of flowers that wants only
to live, be borne again, and then to retreat
beyond the reach of this wandering pilgrim's feet—
Then, oh then, it is only I who am undone.

MARRIAGE

Grief is the crease that disciplines and
divides lover from lover's side, a hot
earthly iron forging a petty truce struck
on the anvil of our clasped, brazen hands.
I understand you in the bridal march from
contention to contentment, shedding
resentments as if all Gethsemanes
were new Edens, measured pennypounds
of all bitter cups not passing you, watched
you touched by Vulcan's fire clutching
your white King James Revised Edition matched
to your patent leather Easter shoes, staring
ahead in the buttock-bruising pews and
wondered, lip-sync-ing John Wesley's blues

> *if the world ever still felt new*
> *to you, as undiscovered as 1492, if you*
> *still see your own eyes Hank Williams' blue,*
> *loving me still just like you used to do.* *

If you breathe the ether of lover's breath,
that bridge is the highest trestle over death.

---

* "My hair's still curly and my eyes are still blue/So why don't you love
me like you used to do?"-*Hank Williams*

MARIE ANTOINETTE GETS ALL GAYED-UP AT THE SUPREME COURT

Now, Supreme Court, I will use my outdoor voice for choices
you made for me. You see, I want to have my cake and eat
it too. I want layers and layers and layers, gooey butterscotch
and groom's cake, too, and I want a pediment love topping
it all. I want it to read, in sediment, "Equal Justice Under Law."

I want my big gay wedding cake decorated in piggish, lardy florets,
one for every corner, and I want it to be so huge that Texas
 women
seeking the heavens by their hair will have a handy subterfuge.

I want a cake so layered that Stonehenge and Stonewall are there.
I want a cake that has a stolen verse of Leviticus curse, and just
more Texas hair. I want a cake with pictures of Jerry Falwell,
either Jr. or Sr.—I don't much care and, well I'd prefer neither.
I want a big, gorgeous ee cummings mudluscious sound of you
putting your hand in mine when I get to marry you after 30 years.

We had no cake.

We had to take the chance we could, at city hall, while the
window was still open. But I'd like my reception, my gooey-butter
cake, and I will still eat cake, whether the Supremes likes it or
fights it. I'm hungry.

A CRITIQUE OF SONNETS

Shakespeare, you're your own jester, or a poor counselor.
Love bends constantly, or it snaps like sugar in the canebrake,
bows each day in these marshy thickets domesticated by decree,
springing tensile, erasing from memory all the stray words, slights
to that fragile and faulty soldered daily repair that improves each
day the grievances it lines out, shreds to confetti, removes. Love
alters every day, and some days it turns the eraser upon itself.
It is not death that parts us, but all the interstitial spaces between
the sugar rows, the intermezzos, when we'd rather carry the
melody forward. We choke on elegant prefixes of love, all thanks
to him, when a simple "I do" would have sufficed quite nicely,
he who left us dumbstruck to learn that suffixes are brutal.

But I'll give the bard his well-earned recompense:
Pardoning breasts of dun is a compliment to common sense.

NEW YEAR'S INVENTORY

I like the ones with Picasso faces,
Angular, not avuncular.
I like the pure strange Cubism
Of a hermetic brain. I like the
Ones who'd raid knowledge
Guarded at Fort Knox. I like a
Shambling walk, the ambling gait.
I like the Atlantic shimmer of
Some eyes, and their shoals,
Too, which sometimes wreck me.
I like their abstract divining. I
Like librarians, taxonomists,
Puritans ill at ease, all painting
These overstrike shapes of a self
That you say you detest—these
Quirks, chin angles, strange colors—
All the strokes that I love best.

GREENHOUSE

There's a woman clinging like
an icicle to your porch.
There's a woman kneeling
in your church, or keeping
her time by your watch.
There's a woman with boots
crunching ice, wanting
scorched August, thinking
twice about you, always.
There's a woman who shivers,
quivering, who never wavers
in this weather, all of it,
for you--hoar-frost
crushing magnolia leaves
we lost. She's there,
malingering the chill on
your tree, one constant
climate, calm, there, still.
One spring-green thing
whenever it's chill.
Calm, calm, calm, so still.

PATINA

The things you forget are the stupid verbal confetti of old love
 letters,
the weight of ancient matters settling the scales of justice around
your shoulders like a yoke or a shawl, and it doesn't matter,
because you're wearing it, for work or for warmth you don't
 know.

They've come to rest there, ploughshares or bodyrags of old
 words,
leaving splinters or growing tattered—it doesn't much matter.
All tales grow old in the telling of them but still are yours, mine,
ours, the dazzling, crumbling libretti of the stars.

We guide the ordinary calendars of intention, calibrate the days,
 paying
a mortgage in years that sometimes feels a ransom for old time's
 sake.
How much dust can rusticate onto sheen, a cherished patina of
 meaning?

I met a dealer in old goods once who told me, copper is a dirty
 metal,
made beautiful by breathing, melding to one ore, oxidizing out of
 thin air.

THE GRAMMARIAN'S ANNIVERSARY OMELET

I know you now. I see you auto-pilot rear view. You
are the driver of all my grievances, my petty griefs,
a sneaky little thief of self until each of us is just one,
but still you're dodging the highway patrol, paying each
freeway toll for me, taking all the bullets meant for me.

My greatest miseries, yours, my beloved, just like Bronte's
warped vision. They float like spores over our jumbled,
tumbled-up lives, a busy and somewhat confused hive
that sometimes seems a little more vinegar than honey.

Honey, curious tourist of all these griefs and grievances,
listen: there's no brochure. But you're still every melting
icicle, glistening, my only relief from a cold, hard winter,
that little splinter bothering memory, and in my greatest

grief, the stark dam against ice and frost—is this love or
did we merely mete a sentence out of dependent clauses?

BABY SHOES

My mother bronzed one of my brother's baby shoes for the
  mantel,
and the other brother's she turned into an ashtray for her
  Parliament
cigarettes. Each was so much older that I saw these as historical
  curiosities.

My wife's feet are not bronzed baby shoes, nor are they made of
  clay.
They are not art nor artful dodgers. They click their heels and we
  are home.

When first I lived with her, in the grace of love's first sight,
  I cherished her
heels kicked off in the hallway, over the threshold, their sideways
  slouch
on the floor as though she were walking in them like John Wayne
  or the
world's most awkward drag queen, vaguely erotic and comforting
  at once,
because they were here, in my space, preserving my comings in
  and goings out.

The night she first woke, later, in my bed, I washed her feet and
  she thought
it Biblical. I thought only that it was cold, and I would warm her
  feet,
which are a perfect American size 7. They have circled me over
  and over.

Now when she kicks her shoes off, they are a stumbling block in
  my way,

a not inadvertent impediment. They are not Cinderella's shoes
 and yet, for
as opaque as they are—not crystal, not enchanted, they are
 impossible to fill.

So I polish them to the best sheen I can, on this, the thirtieth
 anniversary
of that gray-slithered light in a cold house, for her mercies and for
 traveling.

REMAINS OF THE DAY, SPECIAL DELIVERY*

"Neither storm nor rain nor gloom of night
strays these couriers from the swift
completion of their appointed rounds,"
says a New York Post Office keystone,
borrowing from the original Herodotus
and proffered by the 1912 Harvard president
(as edited by the crabbed, palsied, liver-spotted
hand of bloodless and grumpy Woodrow Wilson).
That poem called the Post Office the Bond of the
Scattered Family, which is no Waffle House
Smothered and Covered but then again, what is?

Now I would prefer the silky pop-bluesy version
of Diana Ross and the sibilant Supremes

> *no wind no wind*
> *no rain no rain*
> *nor winter's cold*
> *can stop me baby*
> *no baby no baby*
> *if you're my goal*

But there is no Post Office Lady D fan club and this
is my way of breaking it to you gently that the carrier
left mail saying the Post Office greatly regrets
having lost your mother's ashes and is working

---

* Herodotus speaks for himself. Charles E. Eliot wrote a poem about the
United States Postal Service, "The Letter," referring to the USPS as
"Bond of the Scattered Family," that received some Wilsonian edits.
Ashford and Simpson wrote "Ain't No Mountain High Enough," a 1966
Number 1 hit for Diana Ross and the Supremes ("no wind, no rain.").

quickly and diligently to locate your property and that
it very much appreciates your patience. Please forgive me
while I imagine your mother's ashes flapping over steeple

and brothel alike, shrieking their consternation at gay
letter carriers that you can't call mailmen anymore thanks
to politically correct feminazis and the Jews and the
freeloading illegal people bankrolled by feminazi Jews and
the Jew media and the homosexual agenda that came to
 our house
30 years ago and held a caucus that set up camp and never
 left,
scattering itself everywhere, tossing infectious leprotic
 spores
to waft over churches, brothels, good neighborhoods,
 flying
like spit in the wind, Bond of the Scattered Family.

MY GIRL

My girl is gentle but more shrewd
Than sentimental. A practical,
Even tactical sort, her smile is
A magical cloak over shy ways,
A rushing light in a dark space.

You might not think she's quite
Secure in those bones—no cocksure
Bearing there, just a defiant pure
Resilience. Her eyes are, anyway,
All mine have seen of brilliance.

Once, when we lived on a blind alley
In a gristled part of Irontown,
Three drunk good old boys came round,
Laughing that her shotgun was a toy.
She smiled hard and chambered a round.

My girl doesn't cotton to strangers,
Not that she thinks they're dangerous,
Just meant for crowds, not closer ranges.
She's been nice to those deranged
Unknowns I own by name, just the same.

They think she's ill at ease, a thin reed
To hang heroic arguments from, but
At home, she braves discontents
With a lounge and a smirk, stoic,
Airy and calm as the firmament.

Strangers don't see her, think she's sweet
And weak, the sort who'd turn a cheek

Meekly to the lying Judas-kiss.
They can't see boiling magna beneath
Hardening to a core of igneous.

With her 20/400 vision
She sees what she loves with sharp precision.
Derisively tender, she just might remind us
That only a fool believes his own press,
And we should trust the girl who loves us best.

My girl in a rage is no more than quiet,
A solitary, introspective riot.
But if you could have both oyster and
Pearl, each without the other spoiling,
That generous cloister would be my girl.

PIMP MY PURPLE LOVE COUCH

We called it the purple love couch because it could have been
in Redd Foxx's parlor, maybe surrounded my macramé wall
 hangings
and lava lamps, a pack of Parliaments and bottle of Jagermeister
on the floor—velvet, more divan than couch-shaped, with a slight
nautilus curl to better settle into corners and purr at the room.

When we broke up for what I thought was for good and all, mainly
for good, I had forgettable illicit relations on it and discovered
the couch worked just fine without your familiar profile reclining
there. Years later, your recumbent place restored to its honor,
we gave a little nudge to some cells that would shape themselves
into our daughter, who would decide eight years later to be our
 son.

My favorite dog, from whom we retrieved stray tumbleweeds of
gauzy blond hair from the heart pine floors and chipped stairs,
took up a post there to bark so hard at stragglers on the sidewalk
that she peed on it, piss-stain big as a watermelon. So we covered
it in kitschy faux sheepskin. Then I moved it to my urban renewal
 office

where round-assed rich ladies and willowy interns who made the
 old
round rich ladies feel young and cool by ass-to-couch osmosis
all sat on it, sipping our cheap nonprofit but earnestly felt shiraz—
for the sake of all our unstained politics, and marches, and sacred
 rights.
When they fired me for my increasingly visible disdain for
 nonfamilial
ass imprints on my couch, my regretful and regrettable, shabby
 but some

time ago alluring, Redd Foxx-a-licious, temptatious and capacious
purple love couch came back home to its happy place beneath the
 familiar
windows looking down on sidewalk pukers straggling from bars,
 mail carriers,
people with steaming bags of Thai corner takeout, blessing it with
 new offerings
of dog-voice, piss, and fur. That couch is upholstered, steam-
 cleaned, two-houses-
and-an-office, mohair-blanketed proof that some nothings ever
 change.

YOUR IMAGINARY FUNERAL

Your executor turns away the floral dross
of execrable folk who spurned you.
Your eulogist skewers your nasty boss
who ambushed, burned you without warning.
You direct contributions in your memory
to cross-town rivals in philanthropy.
You stick those bourgeois peace lilies
right in their hypocritical Achilles.
Your dead self toasts from the Antilles.

Another eulogist—for you have legions—
puts the ramparts of some Jesus-crazies
in the very backmost pew, the best places
being reserved for nonhereditary reasons
(such as that they actually somewhat knew you).

At your hypothetical funeral, they say,
it was so nice that FDR died before he retired.
We can remember him signing orders for D-Day,
not playing sponsored rounds of celebrity golf.
Your empanelled dead self scoffs, brushes off
the clay of banal denial, flicks to a mystery TV
channel. We pause a moment now for those monsters.

PRE-MORTEM CODICIL

When I'm ready to be shipped to the shelf like potted
 meat
please don't send me to the lush pastoral retreat
that a name like "Autumn Meadows" wears to assuage
your guilt, assuring you that I am engaged in recumbent
bliss, every fiber, ounce, and cell of my being content.

No, send me to the happy home where all the nurses
ride Harleys to work, or at the very least gnash out curses
to patients whose colostomy bags are not coordinated with
their shoes, who hum verses from Black Sabbath and scream
"Hold your hearses!" Hire for me Bram Stoker's carriage

and may it careen over macadam roads with the rising haze
of dry ice enveloping the wheels and the draft horses' legs
as the music climbs from plaintive minor notes to a crazed
crescendo. Then have the stage cameras cut to fix on one
"Death Cab for Cutie" sticker and let the percherons run.

AMERICAN LAUREATE

I want to be the poet-in-residence at Mall of America oh yes
where I'd ululate, scream, chest-thump and rant and chant
and assemble everyone into drumming circles where we shriek
about our angry vaginas hanging by a thread and The Patriarchy
wielding an equally angry sword of Damocles over our heads
and rhyme and order are prosecuted as political crimes. I'll stage
an aggrieved liturgy like a fly in the ointment of Elmer Gantry.
My polemics will be your poetics, America's little gospel of verse.

This will be cool because St. Paul has lakes where I could ice-
fish for inspiration, spear my metaphors and toss subtle ones
 back.
I'm after the ones who can swallow the whale of protest, wear
 little
berets and yell into microphones. All the good ones got away, and
the little crappie are polishing the tarnished turds they call MFAs.
I'd wax apoplectic, rattling my saber-toothed prophetic jaws
with Hippocratic incision and my kiosk will be ideologically pure
as Windex, right here, right now, at the Grand Mal of the
 Americas.

I want to be a hairpin upturned-lip-sneering, judgy, edgy
 performance
poet, authentic as a mannequin enacting brutal store-window
 choreography
at the Mall of the Americas, dipping a toe, tipping my hat, oh yes
 oh yes oh yes.

SCHADENFREUDE

Schadenfreude is a fine embroidery,
its sepia lace fingering the borders
of memory. You remember your college's
literary mean girls, the ones who lectured
you on your characters' fancy names (while
named things like Colette Alaska Bernoud).
Whose Banty Woods she claimed to know,
New Iberia, a yank of swamp in the Tangiapahoa.
The other two Furies picked on me, too.
One swaggered in a beret with a dirigido.
She was the stepchild of a famous humanitarian
satirist and imagined that she inherited his gifts.
What she got was credibility through osmosis.
"Oh the places you'll go" did pause to bestow
an indie bookstore on a trendy row in San Francisco
for her to hang her gray scarf and beret du jour.

I looked them up—not one publication among them.
Like a cobra eating mongoose eggs, I am smug,
my sad slit eyes drawn to my own selves like a drug.
Mean girls, mean girls, you can push my cart uphill
toward Mrs. O'Leary's dry barn, which is blazing.
This banty rooster has rooted your woods and is grazing,
crowing and cockadoodling over your dusty old quills
stepdad left for your pretentious canoodling.
This bird has settled on your shelf and pecks crumbs from your
 sills.

PROPHECIES

I openeth the tablet and this spaketh it unto me:
Good evening Blank Page Blue Gray Resume

I think of the blank pages Moses dropped so
now we'll never know about the footnotes

bearing equivocative instructions, ghost-inflections,
innuendo of the swirling hurricane breath of God.

The breath of God, original inspiration having collapsed
my lungs, I return to my bed, and the pup curls under

my arm, for warmth, for protection, companionship,
and just as though he were a lover I was loath to disturb

even though my arm fell asleep and I could not,
I let him profile a pillow and burrow all night.

This fulfills the prophecy of the dog Quill.

ANOMIE

Even the squirrel's tail is laconic,
bedraggled in the heat. Sidewalk worms
have wriggled themselves ragged,
writhing into one more ironic
twitch away from the rescuer who'd
toss them to grass. They know the
robins like them juicy, not dried.
They'll die flash-fried to concrete.
Even worms thirst after pride,
spite the predator by dying first.

RESUME OF THE BEST OF INTENTIONS

I offered to be Michelangelo's hand model for his heroic ceiling
but as he painted it God lopped it off and I drew back a bloody
stump. The stigmata of my experience is written on the chapel
 walls,
a little sestina in the long-winded Pentateuch of begattings and
 bygones.

Angry, I bit the hand that feeds me and it coiled up, struck, bit me
 back.
I became an anarchist in the Order of Parliament, saboteur of the
 choir,
a loud provocateur of clouds, a dung beetle crawling on the
 Sunday pews.
I moved to a street where people had good tires so I could slash
 them.

The authorities told me to turn back my clock, so I went to Dealey
 Plaza
and they said that's not what we meant, we use Dali's Eastern
 Standard
Time, except for Indiana where it might be 1963 all the time, we
 dunno.
Panicked, I turned the clocks counter and wound Big Ben's hands
 to 1984.

The People Who Matter began to wonder why I ate my lunch with
 the
Untouchables, began to question whether my adaptation to
 deformity
had made me a little too common, or a little too strange to them,
 because
they were all the Michelangelo models who pleased God. I tried

to appease.

I lit candles, fondled a rabbit's foot I kept concealed in my neat
 pocket.
I was the first investor in a shamrock farm on a reclaimed
 Superfund site.
I put heather over my transoms and recited the incantations of
 the Psalms.
Salted my windows and doors, hung chicken feet and mistletoe in
 the trees.

And still, no luck in sight, I bleed on the chapel walls as God re-
 coils, strikes.

DIRECTOR OF MEMORY CARE

Dear sir or madam (or search committee), I was thrilled
to see the posting for Director of Memory Care clanging
the employment registers I'm ringing up this morning.
I believe I meet the must-haves for this position, being
somewhat fusty myself. I like the smell of old, real
hardbound books on my Globe barrister's shelves
(mainly filled with works no one reads these days,
the passe old laureates who wrote about actual laurels:
A.E. Housman's fleet lads. I know which poets slugged
their stanzas at the Library of Congress. I know that
it was leather-faced Kennedy inaugural reader Robert
Frost who quipped, "Pretty things well said, it's nice
to have them in your head." I can play at Auden and
Yeats with the ardor of a Baptist at Bible Camp sword drill.
I held Wallace Stevens' swig when he swung at Hemingway.
In sum, my enthusiasm for antiquities is not limited to poets
who didn't spew confessional resentment about what it's
like to be fat, or malcontented, or find a zit on prom night.)

I appreciate the well-turned bed as much as the well-turned
phrase. I admire the crisp precision of the military corner,
the coin bounce on a bunk tucked with stiffened tension.
I am punctual and orderly, more a cataloger than a hoarder.
I flatter myself that nothing slips me, that I notice everything.
I like the vaguely picholine, somewhat mollusk-like smell
of asphalt streets after rain just broke a long dry spell;
an odor of forgotten things, like libraries with spiral
iron staircases and metal shelves that crank closed to
seal the collections of relics, cranks that are obsolete now
due to the ranks of plantiffs' bars offering design corrections.
I like the chalky olfactory assault of falling lath and
plaster, the bitter oxide smell of lead sash weights hovering

over 16-pane wavy glass with uncaulked muntins and chunks
of petrified glaze staring out from tongue-and-groove plank floors.
I like the comfortable funk of old leather saddles, saddlebags,
and the liniment hints of paste wax the enviro-Nazis have
vilified. I like the skunky whiff of old wool or tweed overcoats,
and (My Dog Checkers aside), a modest Republican clothcoat
picked over by mothballs and hipsters making frugality chic.

I keep a desk for old Christmas cards from people I liked
in 1982, and I store my photographs on nonacid paper in
dry plastic boxes in dark third-story closets. I preserve things
for the archives of the curious, out of love for the prosaic or
superstition I could not tell you. (I once found a wallet photo
of an infant in the garage of a house newly purchased and left
it be, feeling wrong to touch it. Then when I saw in the alley
its parents, the photo's two faces torn down the middle, I

made a little gallery of the family, reunited in a roof joist.
I felt that the baby was crying for that.) In the garage, too,
I store my archaic skateboard with flint wheels worn slippery,
desiccated bicycle tires, the dry rot of habits to be parked there.
As you can see, I am a capable and compassionate taxonomist
of detritus, a principled custodian of skeleton keys, a fond
rememberer and tour guide of various deciduous lives,
available at your every, and earliest, convenience, waiting to hear.

GOD'S MATH

I.

God loves his golden ratio,
Fibonacci Sequence.
But on this earth below
Our math is the iron law
Of consequence, each birth
Betraying the lover's bed with
Its deadening weight.
Love is made to pay its freight.

Love is heavier than time.

II.

If you are announced voiceless
Who is it pronouncing in me
Your name, evanescent
Petal? That column of light
Where you bloom is yours alone.
No intersecting plane
In all God's arithmetic
Should make this another's own.

This profusion of flowers—

III.

I know my formalities
Stiff as the press-dried tissue
Of habit, hard as the reality
Of hate. I am a grim

Muscle of discipline.

My habits have waxed reflex.

IV.

Habits of command, at any rate.
Listen for a sound like stone
On stone, your disarticulated
Bones clicking into memoried space,
All the nervous, narrow crevices

No one probes, where fractalated
Leaves replicate ourselves, mirrors.
Your bones replace my marrow.

Yellow roses remember red.

V.

What remains either yours or mine
Against the sacred geometry of time
Suspending us like a sublime
Upended garden rending its
Odd contusion of blooms?

My mind bleeds confusion.

VI.

That saint who said it's better to
Marry than to burn yearned only
For God to confirm this: that

All gardens seeded from Eden
To ours aspire to flame,
Conspire with the buzz of clocks
Meticulously unblooming
Them, burst to burn alive.

Unrequited, requiting themselves at last.

DRIVE

I drive my kid to school, friends home
when drunker than I am, drive us all to
distraction or destruction, drive us crazy
with circular ramblings. Ouroboros!
The cul-de-sac of my intentions like
a futile worm trying to aerate the soil
of our fossilized lives: some coal, shale
oil, and just old-school, limestone cliffs.

Take this wafer. You'll want a road snack
later, melting on your tongue as each
memory speaks its own truth, leaching a
budding tooth of wisdom, hollow in your ear.
Communion has nothing on us, old soul!
Here. Let me drive. Give me the clutch
of all your relics, igneous bliss, all your
carefully calibrated curbstones of sediment
crushed by wheels of my machinations.

We will drive past the denizens of heaven.
(They're no citizens of this world, for sure—
extortionists ransoming your dreams and
reading you the obstinate tarot of your life,
Ouroboros unfeeding its tail, card of strife,
telling tales on you.) The fleet magician
in his deck is winking at all your fool's tricks.

Handle, fondle, these pale cards enough,
meditate on the deep question, and then
shuffle with precision so it's not the same hand
you were dealt, but the one of your making. But
if these wheels slip, if we giddily slide on a curve,

if a falling rock or ditch takes us into a swerve,
I know exactly what to do, honey. Gear down, hard.

PEDESTRIAN'S PARABLE

If we bite down hard on bridle bits of indecision,
we still have decided: spitting in the wind of fate
never reconciled wind to fate. But windmills
already resolved this much. This life's a phase
you're going through; you'll outgrow it after
a few decades of wreck and neglect. It will
pretend to forgive you, cuddle you in the
pincer-jaws of hope, then heckle you while
you're on your knees begging for that wafer
hanging over your crib from a knotted rope.

When oxymorons are our tutors of meaning,
we are trapeze artists, pirouetting, careening
through our carelessly edited histories. Still
we master the art of jaywalking on tightropes,
the bastard's grace of stumbling in crosswalks,
tumbling toward that lead particulate of hope.

ACCIDENTAL SHELTER

Even the heretic knows laws of arithmetic.
The pale shadow of a kiss slips a shadow
over our lives; the massed weight of kisses
casts a monumental shade over our graves.
So what was added here, shadows or kisses?

You'll spend your time ticking metronomes
of kisses, hearing these little minuets, our
cartography of breath mapping existence,
and lay still as a flower folding at the moon.

Whatever voice the wind makes the gong
or the tinkling cymbal calling us on, will
shake loose one last kiss, a migratory murder
of crows flying tree to tree, collecting
thistles for nesting. And if you never know
this to be death, a kiss is at best the infinite

accident, resurrecting itself. It never was
your fault. Love is only benign tolerance
recusing itself, grief's briny refusal to let us
judge too soon. Its wreath laid on the vault,
a hallowed relic sheltered by shadows,
tucked away like an orchid, misted by kisses.

TRAMP

There's a dog named Tramp who lives at the gas station
down at the corner, where I go to get my little rations of
Skittles. He doesn't get up for just anyone, but he does
for me. I go there only to see him, unless I want a dose
of pure olfactory nicotine between my eyes, in my nose,
but I want to pat that head of Tramp where he blesses
lottery tickets being sold, vagrants like me wandering in,
customers indulging in ice cream or some other sin.

I know that one day I will come in that door and Tramp
will be no more. My home dogs hate me for my sheer love
of Tramp. They reproach me: "We, too, rise to greet you,"
I know it's their reproof. They sniff me whenever I visit
Tramp, tattooing me with righteous opprobrium,
letting me know with a huff and a turned back that I
am a dog slut, a red Jezebel, the whore of Babylon.
If they could write on my death notice, they would opine:
Tramp, Tramp, Tramp, Tramp, Tramp—but *you're* mine.

And I know, one day I will open this door of our house,
not a grocery store, and an old dog will be spread on this
floor, and no one heard that final whine: "You're mine."

ELEGY FOR A GOOD BOY

No one sleeps when the old dog has died
because he slept in your bed every night,
wrapped like a G-clef to your side.

No one sleeps when the favorite's died.
Your child weeps; the other dog might
die of dazed grief, too. Your child says

I cannot sleep because the dog has died
and he regrets dog days of August, hot,
when we dared not take him walking outside.

We lavish praise on the dumb younger dog,
a maze of buzz-cut topiary in the brain stem;
we love her but she's not him. She dimly tried.

We dream biscuits for the dog who has died,
one more head pat, belly romp, a hot walk,
but we saw his knowing stare, his final pride—
we've seen the "Let's go" glare from eyes that talk.

GODSPEED

I do not ask you to believe
in the survival of personality.
I can only say that old dogs
return, after they die on
Veterans' Day, day of the
first snow of the season when
it's not the snow-season yet.
They send you a meteor
on a not-quite full November
moon and in case you blinked
and missed it, dispatch the follow-up
of an old dog hesitantly
shivering on the street who comes
straightaway and honors your
lonely house with her visit until
the owner of her leash is captured.

You wonder if your dog meant to
send comfort, or do her self-imposed
job of patrolling the parameter so that
no leaf fall or possum pad goes untracked.

***

There was that one other old dog, too,
taking pity on my outsized talent
for grief. After he left he sent a frantic stray
who stopped my smoking breath in mid-
exhale, a blazing star on a chest
otherwise black as Alabama night,
just like the one my Jeremiah flashed.
The streaking dog fixed glazed eyes

before rushing higher up Red Mountain,

followed by a black cat with lightning
bolt of white starring her chest (in case I'd
blinked and missed the stars, the sky the first
time), streaming like a meteor up that high,
high climb. I do not ask you to believe in God
thunder-breath of the universe I do not ask

I do not ask you to believe in anything
but the enduring mercy of meteors, visiting stars.

THE MAGICIAN'S DAUGHTER

"Never ask a magician to do a trick twice,"
she says, the magician's daughter.
Her hands, I think of when I think of her.
Her hands circumscribe miracles.
They weave, in and out, such tenuous dreams
as form my life; they fabricate.

She is the magician's daughter:
mending holes in the air
by stringing ten crystal prisms in windows.
She can mend the tears that the carefulness
of gypsy moths knitting the air cannot.

Her body is a long and brightening star
whose glimmerings and feintings are
a thousand words in diffident signs.

Her trick is this: to make longing chill
my waiting breath, make me a hundred times
stand quiet before Herod and dream
of times dreams were younger (if dreams
be all that bind), and in the silk scarves
of waking sleep, makes me eat
with curled tongue a consummate hunger.

Her trick is growing like a flower
into the soft sweet loam of my soul,
into the soft sweet earth
of me, in some agony of afterbirth.
From both of her bold eyes sprout my breasts,
quick shoots from the early dreaminess of love,
but still, still as death and resurrection.

Her trick is this: hands flying into tremulous birds
beggaring me at my banquet of words
when feeling the curious sympathy of naked flesh
in whose fabric pathos and longing mesh.

It's for this thing she does not guess, this
hat-trick of happiness, splurge of bliss
edged with premonitions of doom, my lips
must know, must wholly kiss her, my flame
in her fixed shadow must quiver, my frail
dreams in those mysterious hands must
spark and shiver, make my slightest syllable
remember tricks she's memorized.

The blood's memory long outlives the brain's.
Her blood will recall someday, settling in heavy sleep,
conjuring bodies shaped like stars cartwheeling off,
remembering laying in the magic box waiting
to be sawed through to emerge only perfect,
flying like a mad rose into the gritted teeth of death:
Resurrected, complete, intact.

Death will kiss her like a dazzling storm,
its lightning flashing free-form.
A flourish of the wrist releasing secrets
or broken bouquets exuding fragrance,
garish petals, a splash of light
in that place where blossoms are crushed by blight.

CHAIN OF ROCK

I will arise now and take myself to the Chain-of-Rocks Bridge,
hyphenated in my head, split by a chain gang down the middle
and parted on its side like J. Edgar Hoover because order just
matters here, and on chains of rocks we may be set free by the
pecking birds at our livers, and maybe, finally, this last thing will
make one last swooping pass, and the hawks come here to nest
and to fatten. And I will think of the TappanZee Bridge, which I
think I never saw but read of in some sad poem of childhood
partings and I will put my car in neutral, the neutral nothing of
all my life dragging me here and remind myself to tell Proust
when I see him that remembrances of things past is just a trifle
redundant, and I will tell him that one book alone was enough
to tell us what Faulkner said, that the past is not Fitzgerald's
prologue; it's not even past—and why did it take more than
one magnum opus to tell you that? And I will be one last child
of the 1960s who stayed awake to see the man on the moon and
not just the man in the moon, a child who learned to live with
the sonic booms of progress, that toxic generational bloom
eating the last tablescraps and then one day in September, no
planes in the sky, and the silence resounding like doom, a
tympanic strain of victories not distant and no, Miz Emily, not
clear, sounding, sounding on the agonized ear, the tinkling
cymbal of a silent war, the "Mission Accomplished" of have no
fear, that hyperbolic acid of words, carbolic little tear. You took
everything, in your age just ten or fifteen years older than mine,
and left me here with eidetic memory for the clacking of trains,
the small acrid blossoms of asphalt opening after a rain, a dull
 buzz
pollinating the senses of chains of rocks, bridges, runways of *was,*
was.

144

BETTY FRIEDAN TAKES A SECOND JOB

There are no porches here so the moms sit on stoops
basking in the Uranian bliss of maternity,
blowing kisses to passels of after-school brats.
There's always one, though, strutting like an imam
on hopscotched-chalked sidewalks, stalking errant
children who are not even hers, picking up
Jolly Rancher wrappers like a prison crewman.
She's got a mechanical arm like those cranes
plucking charms or plush toys at the grocer's door
to tempt the undiscerning eyes and greedy reflexes
of little sprites who, like crows, claw at shiny things.
With it she rends the air in shows of opprobrium,
finger-raking a rebuke screeching like every squeal
of every blackboard even though there are no teachable
moments in a kid's unreachable leisure. There she is,
cumulonimbus of authoritarian purpose,
and just like those sentinels they escaped at half past three,
she's turning over their little taxes thrown on sidewalk temples
to giddy joy, the tithe they pay for unshushed giggles.

The schoolchild's algorithms of the everyday, the accessible
hermeneutics of now make you a walking anachronism in the rain
yanking drooling Cerberus by his chain, splashing galoshes
at your idiosyncratic boss metaphorically spying on your
 downtime,
as grateful as they are for this short afternoon's freedom.
You watch the fecund Horace thundering and rumbling her
 chorus.
Conundrum, you think, a fancy word for making choices
launching a hundred hypocrisies to land us on this block for
 cocktail
conversation. They're called attractive, and a nuisance, for a

145

reason,
just as your keeping of accounts for Scrooge and Marley, LLC,
is called evil, and necessary. There are reasons that we've learned
since our school days, that the children still trip on, skipping rope.

ALGEBRA OF THE ORDINARY

Once you've been broken in by the giddyup of love
It's all: get up, fool, because the coffee sure is.
Your last breathy kiss could be a trip over the snow
boots your child strung last night on stair rails
like Christmas lights. These scraped, pissed up,
dog-bitten, flaking, splintered petty inclines,
this downward climb toward the chirpy-cheery
chime of your microwave marking annunciation
of frozen hash-browned breakfast potato patties,
the advent of caffeinated daily holy water today
discordant, like the disordered anticontextual
boots dangling from stairs, tripping you unawares
in this, your itinerant kingdom of chaotic prayer--
All this, you say, is most assuredly not yours, this
domestic embalming, entombment and mommification.

Giddyup, the fog-breathing carousel horse of Monday
is waiting, Tennessee-walking, stomping, champing
to go. Get up. Get up. There are boots to fit, coffee
to sip, lullabies to put away in the bedside cupboard
of black and bay, dapple and gray, paint, and all the
pretty horses—and who taught you that song anyway
because surely it was not your mother, who never
memorized children's rhymes or doggerel.

Your child, that shiny thing the Fates paused to drop
in your wake-up cup, was left on the revolving doorstep
of this most ordinary day, kicking the stairs sock-footed
in a heavy tread that demands boots, each kick a pang
that ages these creaking steps, settles and unsettles this
old house, rampaging against the ramparts of your sleep.

A VALEDICTION: FORBIDDING COWARDICE

Daughter, bear the slights of the petty with grace
and aplomb. The porcelain smile on your face
will write of itself the pretty words
they'll choose for your tomb, recording
that you chose your battles well.
The rest can fight it out in hell.

My lesson is let plebe and patrician alone.
There's no sport in baiting the very dumb,
and you'll never beat either for influencing
the tilt of the world tilting at windmills—
The stupid are beyond convincing,
and the rich won't roll away your stone.

Mind the manner, not the honor of your word.
Ungreased candor only blunts the sword.
And courage was made for the cupboard.
This world, if no mild place, is the hoard
of the meek. Shh, my girl, don't speak.

Mind your pusillanimous p's, querulous cues.
The world builds altars to the timorous
who are generous in their alliances,
who have the temerity to putsch defiance
and study popularity as a science.
Bite on verity as you would a bullet
at an amputation without ether
and every polarity of man's universe
will verily reverse God's curse
and laud your jocularity.

The meek earned their own beatitude,

won an earth unscorched by thoughts either
deep or divisible, whose worth
is wreaked out in platitudes.
Apocalypse alone is birthed by temper.
Our creation is just a whine and whimper.
Stepchild Truth is no Big Bang, just a birthing
pang orphaned by jackboot ingratitude.

Voltaire knew the law of gratuities we ply:
Live long enough to enrage the actuaries
calculating your annuities. Me, I'd vouch
for the mealy-mouthed backroom schemer
who perches where opportunism knocks,
flattering the acuity of his sense-shorn flocks.
Don't slouch! Lurch! Pluck out the eye
too discerning. By all means be of use—
a churched diplomat, and, if must be, obtuse.
The strong man may covet your ox or your ass,
but it's the dullard sheep who reaps the grass.

MY SON FINDS A BIRD IN THE HOUSE

The bird beat against the sealed chimney
until we could stand his suffering no more
and wondered to ourselves if God is just
or if he's just a god, like Hermes clawing
the air and hoping to draw fire there
to ballast his winged feet up and out;
thought of Poe's pallid bust of Pallas,
heard the little heart and wing thumping,
hovering over the abandoned coal grate,
desperate for flight, for frenzied escape.

I thought then of a communion when
I was ten, and an old man put his thimble
of drained grape juice back in the tray
and mistakenly I took it, saw the snaked
throat straining only afterward, the gray
mottled crop, the pained knees bowing,
then clutching the rail to rise toward
the altar. I was terrified that that sip could
transubstantiate my blood into thick
old-man plasma, brackish miasma
of liver spots and phlegm. I wanted
"This Do in Remembrance of Me" to be
a fortress I could flee, escape from him
straight up to a ravening heaven.

I thought that just two days ago a sister
who always renders news of death had called
to say a preacher cousin I barely knew had died,
expecting that I might care, or even remember.
I expressed the expected degree of distant sympathy
for his pulpit, his family, spent some breath

casting a reel for his wife's name, the church,
but I wanted to let go the line, free myself
from obligatory empathy. I recalled of him only
that he found something or other nice to say
at the lonely funeral of my criminal brother.
This memory gifted me the debt of faint praise,
something my own wife would later that day
remark: "At least he found something nice to say."

I told my son a bird in the house signifies
a death coming to the house, and we freed
it under our roof all the same, he screaming
my name and trying to flee the panicked flutters,
scattering crumbs to lure it out the window.
But first it beat against the walls, flitted to the mantel
like Poe's graceless bird of yore, careening into
the closet door. It made its clumsy escape
and fell into the sky as Atlas shrugged, risen bread
in his claw, a memory of brief indignity.

PLAYING THE DOZENS WITH MY SON

"You are a master of inconsequence."
"What does that mean?"
"A person who thinks he's all that and a bag of chips but who
leaves no impact."
"You mean like a bee-sting on cardboard?"
"Yes. That's marvelous. Can I have it for a poem?"
"*May* I," he corrects. "Sure. I don't like poems or cursive music."
"Ooh, I like 'cursive music,' too. May I have it?"
"OK. I'm going to start a business of making words for you."
"I'd pay you."
"You are a big nasty glob with dried ketchup for a head and flies
lick you—"
Here he looks up to read street hieroglyphics
and concludes with "and you have stop signs for feet."
He offers this up for a poem but I say
nah, save that one for your college admissions essay.

DIPLOMATIC FICTION

The child, straining arms, leverages his haunches onto the chair
so he can haul down a wall sconce, a shiny thing he's been
 coveting.
When I ask who spoiled the plaster, he swears the fair-haired dog
who once bit him when he launched himself from an indulgent lap
unsconced us. Though this rings of a vengeful lie, the indulgent
lap's owner exults that the child has just lapped Piaget's gene

pool like an Olympian and we should effuse praise. "Baby's first
 lie!"
Enthused as a cobra waltzing a mongoose, I mutter, "I see you've
 been
talking to your sister again." Years later, we monitor all his Turner
Stages, send him to the best schools we cannot afford. Well-
 schooled,
he now ferrets out tarnished things and shines his sconce on
 them,
until I grow lonesome in my last ossified bone of habit for
 Piagetian lies.

THE LADYKILLERS ARE SOMEWHAT OVERRATED

A study in Ted Hughes, Frank Lloyd Wright, and Charles Lindbergh

I.

If they're wrapped a little too tightly, an unsprung
coil, a garden hose in any Girl-Next-Door's or yes
prison yard, any small thing held tortuously aloft
in bell jars or cabined up in Fourth of July wrappers,
they're gunpowder in a quiet muzzle, any firecracker
that might be a dud, you'll like that, Ted. Wrap it up.
You'll take it. Those monarch wings, just pinned,
never spreading on your watch. A little match is
all it takes. Butterflies are stupid things anyway,
blooming out of awkward ugly stages, wormy, short-
lived, and they leave traces on your hands once
you've caught them. It's revenge for the touching, the
residue, that leads you both to the gas, isn't it? The
killing space, charnel kiln, and just like gunpowder
these traces of flesh will bond to fingers, these
hands garroting groom's tie, knotting the noose over
your throat, to grace every word Sylvia ever wrote.

They'll knit your socks, your sleeves, smoothe
your collars with a murderous hand, and breathe,
yawn, take in your other wife with Sylvia's glass
in her paws, looking at you, your scrawny lines,
mewling discontents, and all, all, will leave you.
Sylvia will leave her children with milk and their
cereal, Ariel having sealed them off from fumes
like ovens or your poems, or the rumors of your
dismal affairs and sordid self-love. Some tape
outside their doors like Passover blood blocked

this all. But your other wife, with Sylvia's brush
in her hand, her robe cocked over her shoulder,
says of you, Ted, "In bed he smells just like a
butcher." In your bed, two days after Sylvia died,
this is what-will-be-your-new-bride said. In her
bed, this adhesive works in reverse, pinning her
to earth, your last trinket taken, death's afterbirth.

II.

You lay all things horizontal, so nothing soars.
The concrete you pour is all break-your-mama's back
of five squealing children. You couldn't be bothered
with all these good designs squandered, with her,
with them. You built a vaulted playroom way up top
and moved your own mother in next door, to clapboard
yellow rising those three stories above you, looking
down, like Victorians will do. You shut the kids up like
caged birds, because good children are seen, never
heard. They see you, though, these kids, provincial oak
pillars of this grim society, original censors, unbending,
demanding, vile, unyielding, spurning your work.
That town, your drafting tool, a harsh writer one day
will call a place of wide avenues and narrow minds.

You will steal from your mentor, take sly sidework,
trace his designs and call them all your own while he
pays the mortgage for your mother to torment your
wife, fomenting grief all along your low-browed roof.
You've left them no firewood stored against winter.
When your client at Robie House calls you, miserable
in her marriage, miserable with her drainage, with
a leak over her chair because you, theoretical
engineer, don't reinforce anything, since truth told, you

155

take geometry's clarity for structural stability,
convenience for comfort when it's all just stiff as hell,
true to form quite curtly say, "Madam, move your chair."
She lived fourteen months there, in your bricked-in
bunker, hunkering down where your forms failed you.

And after many months of spastic construction, your
temper-fits, an ad-man bought it next and died, and then
it went to a man in trade. None lived in it longer than
a decade, in a time when folks did. It passed to rowdy
fraternity men, and then the seminarians prayed to
finish it off. When the wrecking wheel came, you
were 90 and said of your gaping-maw basement, that
subterranean drawbridge to Levittown and the vaunted
doomed American Century, "This goes to show the danger
of entrusting anything spiritual to the clergy." Well,
they didn't end you that day, did they? Dorms bloomed
for God's dowdy clarions right in Mrs. Robie's backyard,
instead. That's what prayer'll get you: a view of
the squat thing we'd all wreck if wrecker could.

What did you ever rightly finish, Frank? Your Robie
is a dismal, low-slung thing on a cooked plain without
light, a prairie of paving stones even then, with no sky
in sight. Its privacy skulking from basement entry,
its buttock-punishing furniture unlivable, its tiny
eyes massed on a scale just enough to shrink Missus
or make her crazy in the blighted light of Chicago
at any time there, with just the tap of rainwater over
a chair. You never finished anything, Frank, except
Kitty, the kids. Mr. Cheney hired you to build a house
for his old-school brood, and you guilded a low,
sloping elopement with his wife. You visioned her a house,
next, that in a Welsh tongue means poet, magician,

priest, tended and spurned by the unfaithful servant, your
Taliesin. It was burned over the heads of this your
mistress, her dismal brats, but you were away. No axe
or wrecking ball or cocktail of carbolic acid came for you
that day. But you, stubborn hierophant of alphabet blocks,
your mother's son and man to no other woman, went back
to her Spring Green and took her money again, and
rebuilt, resurrected your Taliesin. And like every yearned-for
obsolescent Victorian tinderbox you torched, leveled, wrecked,
ruined by adjacency to your ground-hunkering rhombuses,
it burned. Your aching scorched earth, you built it all, all,
tire/some-lessly over again, and raised another child,
shame/ful-lessly, seamless as dreams, no flagstone to these
 children,
the women who bore them, bore up under your crushing plans,
as though the draftman's hand rendered you blameless.

III.

Anne Morrow gripped the deathstick of joy in these surreal
ethereal planes you once crossed and pronounced you a
chiseled face, a human cathedral, a chordstrike of grace.
It went downward from there, of course, in a long spiral
like the gifts from the sea she collected, each conch just the
knuckles on your hand gripping the controls of an ill-
tilted machine. Did she know, Lucky Lindy, the one
tumbling moment when an embrace becomes a slur, that
lilting tilting wing that belongs to the one bird way up high
that is unsinging herself, her little chest puffed up with her
pride in you as your little temple busily desecrated itself?

You said it yourself, in an engine against the sky you looked
down on earth like God, strode this narrow world like the
colossus Augustus you were. You, Aryan peacock, would

let her clock 40,000 transatlantic miles with you, even for
awhile knocked-up, and then you'd knock her back with
a smile while she listened for wind or the Orient force of
your contempt. Her father, from the House of Morgan, the
well-walled plaza of cozy wealth, loved his children best.

Your bigamous grand-dad, though, left his clan, made you his
pride. He gave you a lean jaw, a trim fit, a certain gaze.
For those he left, wife in an old country or farmhouse,
a chintz curtain flapping like a funeral shroud in the wind,
your Anne was straining to hear. Her buzz is distant, dismal
in your ear, the whine of all mothers, all the instruments
of rote creation. He stole you from that woman, your wife, as
surely as the surgeon wields the knife on all the ancient pain.

What did old Bruno Hauptman take from you, American
Augustus? Anne went down from the nursery because you
would be so, so angry at flying alone again over dinner, and
your misery never was solitary, was it, craving intercontinental
company. Anne would remember later a sickening thud that
must have been your Junior falling to dirt from the window.
40,000 miles, 50,000 dollars later, you wrote your autobiography
of values on Anne's face, she who loved yours. It's all a ransom
deal, isn't it, anything hardening our souls to earth, tying us here
to these women, these withering brats, these nasty stormclouds
of domesticity. They found him just a little bit away in a grove,
your Junior, not far from this house you had made with Anne.

You named your next children, quite literally, Reeve and Land.
They are tethered to this earth of Anne's shifting sand, not
ambassadors, not presidents, just the dull sedimentary
relief of it all. Anne turns, and sleeps off your Nazi dreams,
but those other five scions you dreamt, who called you
Alcibiades instead of Dad, keep one eye open, distantly alert.
 When Mom's sleeping with the enemy, good kids stay awake.

WHAT THE STARS KEEP

The gaudy stars bless us first,
curse us last, confessional-
like, with sacred obligation
pretend that the last smite
on our names is scratched out
with a fiery finger-point.
It's all just haggard old
Damocles haggling over
our time. Whatever you are
told in that curtained booth
you can keep. It's private,
just between you, an inter-
cessory voyeur and your
grudge-ridden biographer.
The cross-dresser in the robe
who sometimes wears hats
in curious shapes drinks it
in and then with cankered
lip, passes you the gilded cup.
Those giddy little church mice
scurrying your prayer closet,
climbing the sleeves of old
hairshirts, pissing them
and calling it perfume.
I dare you, dare you to
make them your pocket pets,
dare you, to the edge of doom.
I dare you to let them rend
your prayer shawl, to find
you a priest without motive.
Your only expiation here is
the pretense of secrets kept.

Small wonder, that Jesus
bobs and weaves, wobbles and
weeps at the penitence we
furtively observe. Contrition
is useless as that spinning wheel
in the mouse's cage, the
exercise of Sisyphus imagining
completion and escape. You
can't absolve the repetitive
frenzied, aimless commotion
of the acolytes, angry villagers
storming Hades with blazing votives.

CUFFS

No one knows you, your casuistry
or habits of taxidermy.
You're Prufrock's receding
hairline writ huge,
this life you're bleeding
out, a subterfuge.
Not to touch the icky-sticky
thing, not to grope
what's prickly to grasp a hope!
There's Pee Wee Herman
on you, a whiff of vermin,
a felon fleeing blazes
in the loins' crowded theaters
where shame's a vibrator.
Holy crap, son, get a grip
on yourself. This morphine drip
you've nursed is hardly a potent
antidote for these rodents
scurrying your veins' sinking ship.
In the blue light where you're fumbling
something vile and alive is rumbling.

Something is tumbling from your dreams.

There's a monster in the closet
There are boogers on the bedpost
and boogey-men who roast
your sheets while you're asleep,
torturing the whole dismal heap
of half-baked secrets you keep
from yourself. There's a pressed
hair-shirt you wear for Mom,

a curdling superficial calm
in that rat's nest you've embalmed.
But Mother knows. She's hung the clothes
you wear, unraveling the sleeve
you sneeze into when seized
by nasty impulse, her monogram of care.

THE CHURCH BELLS RING WHILE YOU SORT OUT YOUR BASEMENT

An old confirmation certificate, in relative tatters, and relatively,
maybe that matters. Or maybe not. You find it, and in your
Orwellian head, recite "Oranges and lemons, say the bells of
St. Clements." As if primed by a brief moment of piety, the bells
of St. Pius (the Fifth) up the street on Grand Avenue give their
 shout:
Yay for God's home team. You think briefly of Hitler's Pope (not
the fifth one)—Fifth was OK as popes go, and just for a second
 think
how cool it would be make up your own name. I would be St.
Pseudonym the Blameless, helper of llamas, defender of the
 abandoned
Oxford comma. I wish briefly that I were Catholic, just so that I
 would
dangle like a participle in purgatory, that I held some remote hope
of redemption just by having to hang around long enough. Tell me
 how this ends, United Methodists, congregational dissidents.
This thing is true of stuff in basements: they store our suspenseful
 discontents.

"So I prophesied as I was commanded: and as I prophesied, there was a noise, and behold a shaking, and the bones came together, bone to his bone." -- Ezekiel 37:7

STYGIAN MIST

Into that wild and ruthless weather
Through distance and darkness
I cannot measure, you are gone.
Gone before first frost shone
On improbable Arkansas.

Autumn slams sepulchral gates
Groaning weight of lost, lost.
In small talk we rape your bones
Petit denouement ("Gone!")—
Chew your words, drink our health
But there's no sustenance in death.

Two tens you carried won't detain
That illoquacious ferryman:
He'll see you buried all the same.

Profane to bargain or to spend
Sacred cost of recompense
For dreamer, heretic or love,
Not by morning star or mourning dove.

So we dress out Granny Weatherall
But "Death will still inform us all."
That house of bone, cave of breath
Keeps strictest calendar with death.

Alive, this shore, we some remain
To hallelujah in the dawn
That makes our broken ramparts song
Where parched Ezekiel yet gropes,
Live long enough to spade our hopes.

And you, if flesh should swell the bone
Resurrect in stars, or earth,
Or stone, still, as before, as since,
Un:-known, -knowable, -reachable, gone.

MEMORIAL DAY

Death loves no shining mark,
Fussy Victorians.
He is all Ozymandias
Weaving garlands of ashes
For Might Have Been.

Death is no verse on stone
But slow, unrhymed cadence,
Not God's trombones;
Just gradients of earth and spade.
The widow's march is to the grave.

Let Death be that "pretty how town,"
Roses strewn here to Equilibrium.
Install Sorrow as mayor
And Regret chief counsellor.
For Death wants his parades.

Give permit to his ordered brood,
And litter the ground in petals.
Still he sweeps just where he should.
This stand will not be denied. The fee is paid.

We would stumble, hands tracing frescoes,
But Death knows his way, is steady
On his mount, a calm navigator.
All orations are ready, decorations
On the ruined promenade immaculate.

On the platform he clears his throat
For his argument with Cain,
Fits and cinches his morning coat

And cravat, and calls the roll.

The God who said let us argue this out
Never pledged to us to change this route.
Pleas for accommodation are vain.
The shovel just comes down again.

This route is marked by what we broke.
Glittered shards and shreds,
Tossed confetti of our hopes
Squashed dull in the trammeling
Like they never knew glistening.

And he sighs and raises the baton
To start the argument we cannot win,
The dull brass march down the boulevard.
His moment came. It will come again.

Take this wilted wreath of ceremony.
The fresh grief of just-plucked flowers
Is your monument here
That marks the hour of this passing
Like flame through antimony.

This is the only monument—
Tarnished sun glinting on chrome,
This anthem that is all refrain
Of Adam weeping the earth for Cain.
Death turns home. He will turn again.

THE LONG WALL*

Things run underground here in the Magic City,
Mining subterranean veins of grievance.
We might scratch close enough to the surface
of pity were we not worrying the foreman
for some little gems of malfeasance.
We ask after that little yellow-breasted bird
we thrust into caverns of our discontent,
and one or two of us might choose to turn back
for that voice, but our carts are lashed to the track.

Behind us, automatic, snaps into place
the Long Wall of memory, sealing then
imploding all. Here I would cramp
if you would bend, make camp wondering
if caged birds ever sing again, and is she
eying us here from Vulcan's terrain, squandered
by cowards who shot her brightness forward,
a surrogate into earth's veins?

Does she wonder this rough took years to make
and how we can reclaim this waste?
Does she know, in this place where grief is grammar
of nothing much, just the lock and hammer
of strange hands firing glamour at your face
in its box, you dressed as if going no further
than church, that this cramped wall is a long, long space
too generous for looking back—a Kingdom's grace? *

_____

* Birmingham, Alabama is known as the Magic City. It is a city founded
on red ore mining, and Vulcan, Roman god of the forge, looms over its
Red Mountain (so named for the ore). Many areas of Alabama are coal
or ore-producing. Long Wall technology uses a machine that literally

170

FISSURES AND WEBS

I.
There I got the call: you need to come home.
I left Jeff City in the tweed suit
I always wore to the Capitol,
my low brown pumps suitable for marble.
It was always the same numbing route.

I had not been "home" since I stood
on the graduation stage and hurled some words
in a sweaty hothouse Little Rock auditorium.

In Cape Girardeau a gravel truck blew a kiss
to my windshield, spreading like a spider web,
spanning the mirror's orange fuzzy dice,
my own personal white trash Rubik's cube.

I checked into a plain room in a sensible hotel,
not wanting to stay at your house in Maumelle.
I'd read the forecast. Maumelle would be raining people
and I'd left my spray-on peoplecide on my St. Louis desk.

Searching the floor for your room in the cancer wing,
I got a sting, a punch in the gut when I looked up
and saw Dad's name, forgetting that we always called you
your middle name. Seeing it there was a shock all the
 same.

---

jacks and supports the "roof" of a mining cave until it is mined out, at
which point the Long Wall machine is removed, collapsing the roof and
allowing the crew to work forward from the mined-out area.

I never knew you'd joined an apocalyptic henpecking
holy-rolling tabernacle on I-67 when you got so, so sick.
People know that death hovers over their voices,
cults of the easily led brain-dead, speaking in tongues.
Your whole family had become a brood of scolds
following the pulpited pied piper I took to calling Brother Jim
 Jones.
They Oompaloompa-chanted some garbled-up prayers.

Your congregation of sanctimonious Kool-Aid droolers
had hung posters in cheery kindergarten colors:
"Steve! You will walk out of here full of Jesus and cancer free!"
"Steve, the Devil will not get you! Jesus declares victory!"
Satan saw a lot of exclamation points in getting behind thee.

I realized that I already have been thinking of you in past tense
and that at least the Oompaloompas know your name.
"He" is Steve. Say his name. Repeat it. His name is Steve.

I whispered to my sister that when you died it would be a rough
surprise; Death had its sting since they didn't pray hard enough.
A gruff nurse in the hallway leaned warily on the wall, tense,
eyes telegraphing that in this crowd I stood out for common
 sense.

She gave me a brochure telling us what to look for on page 13.
I don't wonder how to spell "triskaidekaphobia" on too many
 days.
I thanked her not for my brother or "him" but in your given name.
I recalled again the name of our father leaping from his deathbed
 door
in this very same hospital six full years before. I edit your door.
 Steve.
Your name is Steve. Sing it. Wrap it like a wreath on that closed

door.

Your wife finally agrees to read it, and says it doesn't matter who
  prays;
for weeks she's watched you rending bedclothes even on
  morphine,
embracing earth's tenuous grasp on you while flitting like an ash
  above it.

Briefly, you awaken to suck an orange Popsicle and your eyes grin
  to see me,
even though the whole family knows when I come "home," I have
  given
the hitchhiking Angel of Death a ride through the Ozarks to where
  you'd be.

You say to your wife, "Baby, let's go. Come on. Let's just go on
  home."
She doesn't take your meaning, and pictures the family room in
  Maumelle.
I saw your eyes, your earnest attempt to rush into the yawning
  tomb.
I took your meaning about leaving that prison bed, understood
  very well.

Now that your wife has read page 13, she is willing. The watch
  drill begins;
the med techs on death duty, like so many wind-up soldiers,
  goosestep in.
They try to lift your dragging arms, already dead weight. They are
  too rough.
They want to flip your inert cinder-block body to tape-strap a bag
  to your butt.

I cry out, "You've already torn his rotator cuff." They give me a
 dismissive huff.
"He's not a carriage horse. This can't be how you people manage
 this stuff."
They argue some more before the words "charge nurse" bring a
 shrugging retreat.
They didn't mind being rough with the near-dead. They just
wanted clean sheets.

I go with my sister to the bathroom down the eerie fluorescence
 of the hall
and Pastor Jim Jones seizes the chance to evict one of your
 daughters, your sister
and me from the orderly prosecution of the death order. The
 machines dance off.
The blood pressure plunges below 50. I am allowed back for the
 last sighing breath.
I am flying, now, with you, straight into the vortex of the people-
 storm of death.
I think of my stepsister's house because Steve's house is far too
 people-y for me,
and the air stiff with the widow's resentment of my parents. I
 sympathize in silence.
After 35 years she's entitled, just as I have been entitled
 for 20 years give or take
to not come "home," unless dragging along the unshaved
 vagabond, hitchhiker Death.
Dad, this is my friend Death. Do you want to shake Dad's hand?
Give Mom a kiss?

She's entitled to umbrage at a man capable of squandering breath
 on sobriquets
for his otherwise neglected spawn. I, so much younger than the
 others, an only child,

almost, was the smart one, Susan the sweet one, Phyllis the
skinny one, and Marilyn the sexy one. He omitted the
schizophrenic one among his prawns. You, Steve, who
worked side by side under his name—your name, too—looming
over the highway
like a colossus, he pronounced with faint praise "the best truck
man in the Southeast."

The beast used to brag that when he cruised home in his dealer
car and drove up
by the house, past the windows, we all were lingering, so anxious
just to see him.
Someone, sick of his pride and pretense to our love noted that
6:30 was the hour to sup.
Such tender vignettes trace the contours of "home" and the
fractious family it contained.

You are dead, Steve. When I called the Skinny One I knew that
Death
had stolen my voice, a petty theft. Unable to speak, I drove to the
Skinny One's people- free safe place instead.

The rest of them, people-ing easily with each other at your house
on Lake Maumelle,
glare at my betrayal when I come by to join the meeting of the
People's Temple
planning the funeral, which is to say listening to the First of the
Seventy-First
pour out of the thundering pulpit of the Reverend Jabes
Branderham's Brontean
eternal curse on our quest for the Jonestown Kool-Aid, on our
furtive death-thirst.
What a fine Pimm's Cup he nurses.

Steve's Jack Daniels is tantalizingly high on a shelf that is far
   beyond my parched reach.
I said my piece and left, knowing later they'd spread my bones on
   the gossip platter.
"So aloof," they'd say. "We've got plenty of room for her to stay
   right here with us."
"So cold-natured. I guess now she's a lawyer we plain folks just
   aren't good enough."
My family has always been woundedly, huffily, gruffly expert at
   carving the meat
clean down to the bones and then painstakingly ragpicking the
   tortured carcass.

At your funeral, my four-year-old asks, "Does this mean Uncle
   Steve has gone to God?"
"Yes," we rush to assure him. "Yes, he has." The Skinny One smiles
   and takes my hand.
A cousin I'd never liked stayed for the burial and made everything
   go too people-y.

We sang your favorite hymn, "Great is Thy Faithfulness," I again
   in my prim tweed,
and I peered through my cracked windshield in the cortege,
   knowing I'd never replace it
because it was a sentimental web. The fissure spread until the car
   was taken in another theft.

***

But blessings for the wingnut, for the Oompaloompah Greek
   Chorus shrieking dissent.
Give us the wretched refuse of Gulliver's teeming shores and hurl
   them at Arkansas.
Blessings on each and every carefully numbered, God-forbidden,

176

cult-ivated head.
Look for me rising through Ozark fog with vagabond angels
  shedding themselves on 67.

II.
Great is Thy Faithfulness O God my Father
There is no shadow of turning with Thee

Shalom. I am not Jewish.
May the road rise up to meet you. I am not Irish.
Peace be with you. (And also with you.)

I was told to take no home communions or I would surely die.
But I recovered, and lawyer-like, told myself that three
airport wine snifters aren't at all like a fifth of vodka on the shelf.

This, unlawyer-like, makes me an Idaho prize rutabaga
or just a plain old Southern hypocrite. It's your pick.

I awake after surgery with renewed urgency,
my eyes glazed with new paints ordained
for my Doric columns of blessing
to hold them aloft, grateful for the glitterlujah
and the whirring waterfalls of the skies.

> *All I have needed Thy hand has provided*
> *Great is Thy faithfulness Lord unto me.*

Bless me, unscale my eyes to recognize blessings.
Unsuffer me so I do not wander unjustly in the way
of Jacob or Esau's numbered hairs awaiting a blessing.
Let them each have their father's blessing.

Blessings on me, sesame to thankfulness.

Blessings on drunk drivers who give us partial criminal livers,
dangerous little slivers of the whole.
Bless our nostrils with petrichor after our long dry spell.
Blessings on me, archway to gratitude.
Blessings on all of us, new owners of criminal livers
and the hands that pried the wheel from the giver.

He is risen, Allellujah.
Oompaloompaly, He is risen indeed
in the basements of United Methodist churches.
He is risen to a new creed. Oompalujah!

We trudge our meandering way through the Stations of the Cross
 we bear.
But bless our beastly criminal-liver hearts that got us here.
Throw shade from our Doric columns of gratitude back at us
but bless us anyway, our leaking, hypocritical breath
panting out its exhilarating courtship with death,
until one day we savagely, sadly, marvelously cease.

Amen. Gratis. Finis.

THE PATIENT IN ROOM 327 HAS TOO MUCH AND TOO LITTLE TIME ON HER HANDS

i.   On Why I Broke Up with Siri

I broke up with Siri because she asks too much and I want too
much.
"Can I help you?" she mechanically purrs, and I, cursing her
efficiency
over the whirr of the oxygen tank with the asthmatic lady in the
next bed,
want to poke at Siri's deficiencies. I ask where the nearest
whorehouse is.
Siri, her coded confidence shaken, insists that "the nearest
courthouse is. . ."
I asked Siri why the host at the fifth damn Thai restaurant to open
on my block
seated that avant-garde couple who spoke not one word to the
other but the man
stared at her plate, watched her wordlessly take in a flaccid
taupish pancake
atop her noodles, resentfully begrudging her dainty little neck its
prim swallow
as though he were a one-man Navy Strike Force against the "Me,
Too" women
scamming and skimming him on the dinner check and tip while
dabbing her lips.
For this Siri had no answer, again. But I know, Siri. I know this was
no swan song
stuck in her throat, just a mumbled cry. Their eyes locked in a
brief, "Just don't
say it" censure. I avert my own because I cannot afford these
homicidal debentures
on the pay-as-you-go menu. Siri, you spoke in too many facts,

when parables would do.
I have to speak up, Siri, and be candid with you. You're truthful, so
I broke up with you.

ii.   On Watching My Wife Learn I Am Dying

I put my hand up to warn you off tears.
I put my hand up to surrender like sometimes
I do to ward the dog off, but he bites my finger.
I put my hand up to salute things that demand loyalty.
I put my hand up, with its band, proof of a wedding.
I put my hand up to pledge allegiance to these broken parts,
and I put my hand up to say no, a futile resistance.
When it's just one finger, you'll hold it up and say "Me, too."

iii.   On Watching My Child Learn that I am Dying While
        Thinking of Hands

Now that the bloat of bile pins me to my bed like Eliot's
 conjecture pinned
and wriggling, using my blankets as a handhold to drag myself to
 the toilet,
grasping for any rooted place to help me rise from this tortured
 white space,
I remember you as an infant striving toward nothing but some
 shimmering,
glimmering mobile, to no purpose but with fierce and noble
 intentionality. You
clasped it with your tiny might then. Hold it as closely now again
 and tell them all,
I am Ferdinand the Emperor, and I want dumplings.
You shout this. Don't whisper.

iv.   On Thinking Back and Knowing You'd Known All Along

There are lines that can't be written.
There are lines that can't be crossed,
like the secrets we're forbidden,
like the sheets we tossed in the sad
lost sleeps of our churning dreams,
wondering if Jesus is angry in his trousers
and his potent justice is coming for us.
That must be the reason for All of This.

In All of This we breathe through the simple air
that's more or less, best or worst, I guess,
poor, rich, the perfumed ether of a prayer.

In All of This, in every hidden place
there is nothing, nothing to me, just ghosts
except your face, that emblem embossing
every grace, each layer of you my fingertips
might trace. If I had only one thing to remember
it would be that day of your curious life cross

ing this one, slow and slack as only a Southern
girl could be, spindly and resilient as Alabama pine.
A vulgar instinct to utter, whatever you may be,
I want it to be mine. Your profile on a pillow, face
at rest, may be the best poem I've seen, a divine nest
of hair, unkempt, unparted, briefly lost in peace,
not worrying about me, your face unlined in sleep.

I foretold these piddling lines you became; I saw
the last rose in autumn. I saw the last leaf, too,
wrestling with winter's edge, sprawling these seasons'
spans from my naked lunch to immoveable feast, saw

these beasts beating you down with every needle
martyring my blood, bruising my veins, you wearing
me like a hairshirt for licentious priests at last suppers,
table for 13, and a few million guests in the Upper Room.
The Lord God of Hosts will seat you with all the rest
presently, when the season changes, but that's not just yet.

I saw, saw you falling tenaciously as a laceleaf of snow,
mettle-testing the dull, dry ground that breaks undertakers'
 backs,
saw you straddling that one last hedge to proofread my
 headstone,
saw tears like holograms tumbling like ice-locked bees stinging
you through the looking glass, darkly—your weeping a slow-
moving squall of swarming griefs. I saw you, saw you tumbling,
throttling over that ledge looking for me. This time, don't follow.

    v.   On How You Regret Important Questions You Didn't Ask
           Siri or Dr. Google

About *Tristram Shandy* and that blank page—was that more
 satire, or
just printer's error? Did Edwin Stanton say "Now he belongs to
 the ages,"
as sage biographers claim, or "Now he belongs to the angels?"
What wire was misguided in Newton's noggin when he stuck a
 bodkin in his
eye to see if blood is really red, or just conjured into color in a
 Newtonian head?
I've had enough needles shoved in me to tell him blood really is
 red, but
I'd still like to know how Siri would program-ponder out this
 mystery.
Why did Aesop go after the low-hanging fruit and then grouse it

was sour?
Why does the loss of your own beauty ring in the mirrors of your ears?
These are the things that keep me awake, however few and ill-spent the hours.

ETERNAL SOLILOQUY FROM ELMWOOD

This plot of ground is a bruised and battered soil.
It contains the worm-tossed remains of one
Helen K. Alexander, who was my Southern
Gothic mother. Jerry, my brother, is butt-up on her stone,
though we all know that Jerry was the one
who very likely broke her neck. He uneasily rests
in a plot owned by my aunt, whose name was Justice.
She gave it because, like most of Jerry's plans,
his VA spot poof! mysteriously disappeared, just as
when he talked your grandmother out of her last
dollar, and the last dime of that dollar slung itself
from his pocket onto the counter of a tavern
and not a cent of it into businesses he said he ran.
For him, either a bar or this simple "Justice" stone
would have been an appropriate retirement home.

She's buried here in the iron-making Magic City,
the Big Bad 'Ham that's practicing gritting its teeth
until that day we all come to Elmwood's rusty gates.
My mother's life rushed by in a breathless, gushing whoosh,
with the crushing velocity of a locomotive engine.
She shrieked her truth about how my father drove 500 miles
to shake the trees and loosen their hardheaded leaves
after she'd just this afternoon raked the yard and garden
and how my father's feet stank "like nothing in this world,"
maybe like a mummy's would smell if he were unfurled
in your living room with its plastic-covered mohair couch
and how a lady is known by her posture so don't slouch
and don't ever sleep with men boys you're not married to,
and go easy on the rouge and never smoke or spit on the street
and don't pop that gum because everybody knows that's trashy
too. . .

On this plot of ground, this raggedy patch of Elmwood Cemetery
she still is chattering her eternal grief and lingering query
of why Aunt Inez had them sneak in and bend her up and take her
to the Place when she'd never been sick a day in her life
and even if she was it was your stink-footed, tree-throttling
 father's
fault. He put her in this vault as surely as he'd made her a nervous
wreck and himself broken her neck. About three yards across an
 asphalt
path, the lady under the mushroom headstone turns in her sleep
and, next to her, grizzled ol' Bear Bryant rolls, shivers, and creaks.

ON THE FRESH MORNING OF FORGETFULNESS

On the fresh morning of forgetfulness
you will bloom numb regrets for all that you do
not know, with the ecstasy of a crocus
taunting the still-buried bulbs not yet awake:
their memories, like yours, snaking their dreams.

On the fresh morning of forgetfulness
you will not know tears from an ocean,
except for that certain fathom of salt
marvelously dissolving our separate selves,
not know even gemstone from millstone,
not know which words to call your own.

You will not cipher what from *is*, on such
a precipice as this. On the fresh morning
of forgetfulness, you will walk limestone steps
of museums, courthouses, coliseums, monuments
to muse the mimesis that framed us and
threw away the key, telling yourself these steps

will lead you to the place that spawned and tossed
us, feel the spray at last on your cracked lips,
yearning for the vast, impervious, enduring sea.

Pamela Sumners has practiced constitutional and civil rights law, with a special interest in religion cases. A native Alabamian, she has worked for the ACLU as a volunteer lawyer as well as staff counsel and director of the LGBT, AIDS & Civil Liberties Project of an ACLU affiliate. She is known internationally for litigating against Donald Trump's lawyer Jay Sekulow, Supreme Court aspirant Bill Pryor, various far-right think tanks and extremist evangelical groups, and a Governor who argued that the Bill of Rights doesn't apply to Alabama. She led the Missouri affiliate of a pro-choice organization with an unpronounceable name for 10 years.

For the past few years, she has devoted herself exclusively to writing, becoming an award-winning poet whose work has appeared in dozens of journals in the US and abroad, won or placed in several competitions, and appeared in several anthologies. Her first chapbook, *Finding Helen*, is a Rane Arroyo selection from Seven Kitchens Press (forthcoming).

She once wrote an eight-page poem with the golf-tee pencils intended for an offertory envelope. (It's here in this book.) She lives in St. Louis with her wife, teenage son, and their rescue dogs. *Ragpicking Ezekiel's Bones* is her first collection.

Praise for the Poetry of Pamela Sumners

Pamela Sumners' work draws the reader into a very personal space with a fine-tuned and musical sense of rhythm in her lines. I'm often surprised by her poetry as she delves into these deeper connections with a quiet passion and grateful that as a reader, I'm offered the opportunity to join her. –**Mare Heron Hake, Poetry Editor, Tahoma Literary Review**

All the world's a poem for Pamela Sumners. In **Ragpicking Ezekiel's Bones** she practices what might be called "the poetics of inclusion." How to get everything in . . .is the challenge she sets for herself, and **Ragpicking** is all the proof I require that she is way more than up to that challenge.
Sumners' work is "immodest," in the highest and best sense of the word, and ambitious, an increasingly rare virtue in an age of small poems. She writes "large" poems, poems that "contain multitudes." She manages, somehow, to get all manner of folks into them, and all her "folk" have stories to tell, stories motivated by desire, by "urgency and longing"—the same motivation that readers should bring to her book.
The reward for such readers of **Ragpicking Ezekiel's Bones** will be memorable, even indelible, lines and whole poems that will not let you leave them, that will stay with you and stay with you, all your life."—**William Slaughter, editor of Mudlark: An Electronic Journal of Poetry & Poetics** and **author of The Politics of My Heart** and **Untold Stories**

Sumners'. . .words start warm, pour on a disturbing heat, then spill blood before looping back into a cool, almost arctic end. . . . Just take care that you don't get hurt.—**Sunshots/New Millennium**

The great thing about Pamela Sumners' poetry is that it takes you to unexpected places—away from the cliched and predictable. Her subjects are many and various; her treatment of them is individual. This is poetry for people who think.—**George Simmers, Editor, Snakeskin Poetry Blog**

Pamela Sumners' work has been published internationally. She was selected by Halcyone/Black Mountain Press for both 64 Best Poets of 2018 and 2019 anthologies. Her chapbook, *Finding Helen,* winner in the Rane Arroyo Series of Seven Kitchens Press, will be published in 2020. *Ragpicking Ezekiel's Bones* is her first full collection. A native Alabamian, she now lives in St. Louis.